Get It Done!
The Simple Process for Finding Harmony by Destroying Your To-Do List

Belinda Goodrich

G⦿ODRICH
PUBLISHING
DISCOVERING POTENTIAL

For information address Goodrich Publishing, 2550 W Union Hills Dr, Ste 350, Phoenix, AZ 85027

Goodrich Publishing books may be purchased for educational, business, or sales promotional use. For information, please email Info@GoodrichPublishing.com

Published by Goodrich Publishing

Phoenix, Arizona

ISBN-13: 978-1-7323928-9-2

Library of Congress Control Number: 2020930337

DEDICATION

When the thought of this dedication came up, there was only one
clear and obvious choice.

Kim, you are my person.
You have stood by me through everything and I know you always
will, without fail. I will always stand with you without fail.

2019 sure did a number on us, didn't it? But we are the Phoenix,
and we rise. We are stronger, smarter, and happier through the pain
and suffering.

I can only begin to imagine the adventures we are going to
experience in the future.
And we've earned those adventures. Because at the end of the day,
we genuinely know how to get shit done.
I love you!

P.S. You're Negative

TABLE OF CONTENTS

PREFACE

It seems that nearly everyone I talk to, regardless of profession, gender, economic status, or education, tells me, "I would be fine if I just had more hours in the day."

That statement, however, is inherently tragic. We would be fine if only the impossible will occur. Because of course, the reality is that there will never, ever be more hours in the day. We are making a desperate request for an impossible outcome.

We are facing a productivity crisis, both in our businesses and in our homes. Our always-on lives have created a tsunami of distractions that have zapped our energy and pulled us in a million directions. And the product of this crisis is a devastating downward spiral in our health and wellbeing.

Addiction, obesity, anxiety, depression, suicide, and stress-related illnesses are at an all-time high. And it's not just our health. Accidents are increasing due to distracted driving thanks to our obsession with our cell phones.

An article published in the Washington Post in 2019, reports that the combination of these is "driving down overall life expectancy in the United States for three consecutive years."

Consider that for a moment. We are living in the most technologically advanced time, yet, we are dying younger.

This book is not just about getting more done. It is about getting more of the right things done, at the right time, in the right sequence, to lead a more fulfilling life personally and to bring about financial and business growth in our organizations and personal health and wellbeing in our homes.

The world has changed, and that pace of change is only getting more and more rapid. Information is firing at us non-stop, and our brain is not adept at managing the flow and prioritizing action under these increasingly challenging circumstances. The result is paralysis and an inclination to choose the path of least resistance: activities that are easy to accomplish or those that are more pleasurable.

The lack of progress, however, towards those essential and critical tasks creates a churning cycle of frustration, despair, and hopelessness. Which, in turn, once again, leads us to choose simple tasks and those that give us pleasure. And so on and so forth, the cycle continues.

I started this book from the point of personal desperation. I was exhausted, run-down, frequently sick, and completely unhappy with my life. From the outside, I had what some would consider a pretty perfect life. I was running my businesses; I took vacations and traveled the world; I had a loving and healthy family. I was continually achieving: more certifications, more publications, broader audiences.

But inside, I knew that it was not sustainable. I feared that my hectic, always-on, high-stress life was going to kill me eventually. I began aging faster and faster. I became a passive observer to an erratically out-of-control life. I was educated enough about human physiology and neuropsychology to realize that this seemingly perfect life of mine could kill me.

So I stopped. I stopped saying yes, started saying no, let go of my guilt, and started making radical changes. I finish this book from a place of health and happiness. I am stronger, more focused, and more content than I have ever been in my life. I want to give you this gift.

The market abounds with self-help books, organizers, planners, productivity software. Yet none of these can fix the problem. If anything, they are exacerbating the issue. These external tools give us hope that we can change our lives and our environments. Yet, when they do not work, we plummet into frustration and despair. We beat ourselves up. We propagate the self-fulfilling prophecy that we are not productive, that we will never change. Trust me, I was there!

Why is that? These external resources are merely providing an external solution to an internal problem. You could have the best planners in the world, but if you have not changed the way your brain is wired, you are merely giving Tylenol for a brain tumor.

This book is different. The process outlined in the following chapters is based on an understanding of the inner workings of the human brain, motivational theory, and the evolution of our information-overloaded society.

I will walk you through a nine-step program to re-train your brain and change how you approach your daily life. You will be happier, more fulfilled, and ultimately have increased life satisfaction. You will rest easier, find life to be more peaceful and less stressful, and ultimately enjoy more time to focus on family, friends, and hobbies. And we could all use that, right?

As a business owner, leader, or manager, engaging your employees in this program will completely change the dynamic, health, and atmosphere within your team or organization. A healthy and engaged employee is, without a doubt, the most valuable asset you can have.

This book has the power to be completely transformational. As with any transformational concept, however, it is only as good as the consistency for which it is applied. Simply stated, I can lead you to the water, but you need to make an effort to drink that water. I will continually challenge you to truthfully examine your life and make a conscious choice about your desire to change it.

Here is the reality: these steps have the power to change your life dramatically. But the effort you put forth is going to be directly proportionate to the results that you receive. Be ready to put in the work to reap the incredible benefits that a more fulfilling life will bring you. Change cannot possibly happen where we are comfortable - being uncomfortable means that we are truly making meaningful change. So let's commit to getting uncomfortable!

Your journey begins in the following pages.

Yours in health and wellness - *Belinda*

Belinda Goodrich

INTRODUCTION

I was recently talking to a friend over Facebook messenger, comparing notes on our new Peloton bikes. I explained that lately I have not been able to ride as much as I would like because I have been focusing on getting this book done. And I've been working on my Neuro-Linguistic Programming (NLP) and hypnotherapy certifications. And of course, it is the holiday season, so I have been enjoying special activities with my daughters and grandchildren.

"I'm not sure how you do all that you do!" she exclaimed. "And stay sane and happy."

Sane and happy. Yes, I suppose today I am very happy. Sane? Some may debate that! My road of non-stop overachievement is rooted in an unhealthy series of experiences and subconscious programming. It has taken me 50 full years to bring it into the almost perfect balance. I will say *almost* perfect because there is always room to grow, change, and improve.

For all of my later childhood and throughout my teen years, my parents owned a business in a small, rural town in Maine. My mother and stepfather were hardly the warm and fuzzy kind, especially with my siblings and me. The irony in this was that their business was a childcare center, and they adored the children they cared for there. (And that is another story for another time).

The expectation on me was that I would work every day, work hard, and not complain. If I wanted new clothes or a new pair of sneakers, I had to earn money for them by working at the childcare center.

My means of comfort came through escape in two forms. When I was not working, I was either in the woods or lost deep in a book. In both settings, I was free to be creative and explore. I loved it. To this day, my happiest times are being in nature or curled up on the couch with a great story.

I did not hate working. Honestly, you could say, in some ways, I *enjoyed* working because I did not know anything different. It was not a punishment; it was just what you did.

When I got pregnant at 16, there was only one option: to work harder because now I was working for two. I managed to maintain a high G.P.A. throughout the remainder of high school while working and caring for an infant. I ended up graduating a semester early, with all of the necessary credits.

My second and third daughters came along by the time I was 21, all three were beautiful surprises. Shortly after the birth of my third and last daughter, I escaped an abusive relationship. That relationship left indelible and damaging scars within my subconscious.

In part, due to how I had been raised and in part due to my stubborn pride, I refused public assistance. Instead, I focused on working my ass off to support my girls. That is just what you did. I am not bragging. I am not judging others that are not able to do this. I am merely explaining that this is how I was wired. I never threw myself a pity party. I just did what needed to be done.

I went on to earn my bachelor's degree in behavioral science, climb the corporate ladder, raise three amazing daughters, achieve six Project Management Institute credentials (the first woman in the world to do so), earn my master's degree in industrial and organizational psychology, and build successful companies. I continually defined my value by my accomplishments. On paper, I was a freaking superstar.

But at what price?

My inevitable and ultimate collapse occurred in 2013. One of my newer businesses, a restaurant, was a massive failure. (I later learned to call that experience *feedback* and not define it as a *failure.*) I only had one friend that lived 2,700 miles away. My marriage was on the rocks. And my health took a significant turn for the worse. Honestly, the collapse had been building throughout my life. And then just one day, the dam broke. I had no joy. I was exhausted, unhappy, and honestly, death seemed like a viable option to get some sleep.

But as the story goes, I did not die. I very slowly and steadily built myself and my life back up. It did not happen overnight. It has been a steady process of evaluating and considering everything in my life and examining how it was serving me. There were no longer any failures, just feedback: cues to tell me that I needed to adjust my thinking or behaviors. I continued to make changes in my life, some small, some huge until I felt this wonderful sense of alignment with my heart and soul.

It is a precarious and delicate balance. I still battle the belief that my self-worth is, at least in part, measured by my accomplishments. And truthfully, I still love to work, I love to achieve, and I absolutely love being busy. But now I do things out of love for myself and a deep curiosity in all things inspirational, psychological, and motivational. Ultimately, I want to serve others.

This book is the result of this massive realignment. While the original thought was that I could simply share my productivity hacks and how I got shit done, I realized that I would be remiss if I did not give you the entire picture. I needed to pull back the curtains and be honest and transparent about my journey.

Your value is not defined by your accomplishments, your title, the number of social media followers you have, or your income. It is time to step off of the damn hamster wheel…. Going around, around, and around, and yet, not getting anywhere. It is time to take back your life, get more of the *right* things done, and ultimately find your joy and fulfillment.

With that in mind, I must start at the root cause of our current state of affairs: your brain.

Our Simple Complex Brain

To fully understand how to get stuff done, how to decimate the to-do list, and how to go to sleep at night feeling accomplished, we need to get to the root of the problem. Often, people will blame their circumstances, their personalities, their lifestyle, their spouse, their children, their job, their demands, and a bunch of other things for feeling overwhelmed.

I'm going to be real with you. Life does not happen TO you. You and only you are entirely and 100% responsible for the life that you have and the choices you make. Step away from the tendency to blame and let's dig down to the core of what is really happening.

Your brain only weighs about three pounds and is intriguingly complex and yet beautifully simple at the same time. We cannot possibly challenge our productivity without a strong understanding of how it works.

We are biologically wired with one principal and primary purpose: it is to survive. It is the ultimate drive of any being, and it supplants all other desires, wishes, and dreams. It is rote and autonomic. It controls our natural drive to move away from pain and move toward pleasure. Survival will always be the primary drive, meaning that when faced with a choice of moving away from pain or moving towards pleasure, we move away from pain first.

Pretend you are cute little bunny rabbit hanging out in the Sonoran Desert of Arizona. You find a nice little patch of grass and are happily munching on it when all of a sudden you spy a coyote in the brush. He is looking at you and licking his chops.

Without even realizing it, your little bunny brain picks one of three options:

1. I can run away from the coyote

2. I can fight the coyote

3. I can freeze and pretend I'm dead and try to trick the coyote

The unconscious mind of the bunny knows that he is not going to be able to fight the coyote, so scratch that option. His cute little bunny brain then weighs the options of fleeing versus freezing and acts accordingly. This all happens within a millisecond.

We are not bunnies. And there is no coyote waiting to attack. Yet our human brains are still operating in the same manner. The only thing that separates us from our little bunny friend is one additional component of our brain missing from our animal friends: the neocortex (our conscious and logical brain).

And yet, while we have this beautiful neocortex, the vast majority of our actions and decisions are rooted in our subconscious, which is no different than that sweet little bunny. You see, as fast as the world has progressed, our brain has not caught up. It is still cranking along, convinced we are on-guard from threats.

And the crazy thing is we do not even realize it. While the core of our brain is functioning at a pre-historic level, our inputs and exposures are of a modern society with increased technological capabilities and unrealistic demands for our attention.

It is truly no wonder that we are more stressed, more depressed, less healthy, and less fulfilled than ever before. These technological advances that at first glance should make us happier and more profitable are only burdening our brain capacity with too many choices, too many options.

The Wiring

When you understand the core of your actions, reactions, feelings, and patterns, you can then seek to modify your outcomes. This is why so many techniques and approaches to improve productivity on the market today are feeble attempts, at best. Instead of looking at the productivity issue intrinsically, both physiologically and psychologically, these solutions are extrinsic, such as planners and apps. They will not fix our productivity issues until the brain has been re-trained to work in our modern environment.

Our brain is a finely tuned machine. Everything we do, experience, and feel is the result of messages flowing through three distinct areas of our brain.

- Our brain stem
- Our subconscious brain
- Our conscious brain

The Brain Stem

What do you and a rattlesnake have in common?

Other than you are both complete and total bad-asses, you have primarily the same brain stem.

It is the brain stem that keeps us alive and functioning. Because our brain stems are similar to those shared by all creatures, it is often referred to as the "reptilian" brain.

The brain stem controls all of the body functions that happen without us thinking about it or controlling it. For instance, your heart beating in your chest, your lungs actively taking breaths, your throat swallowing, your state of consciousness, and even if we are awake or sleepy.

Try to stop your heart from beating, your lungs from breathing, the goosebumps you get when there is a cold breeze. I guarantee you that you will not be successful.

With no external control, the brain stem communicates with our body systems based on messages received from our limbic system.

While we cannot control our brain stem, we are going to learn how to control the flow of messages that the brain stem receives and acts upon.

The Subconscious Brain

Like our friend, the bunny, we have a subconscious brain. In some sources, this is also called the unconscious brain. We can thank Sigmund Freud for that. He bounced back and forth between calling it the unconscious and subconscious. For the purposes of this book, I will refer to it as the subconscious brain. Because unconscious gives the impression that we are completely zonked out, but in actuality, our subconscious is cranking in the background 24/7.

This subconscious brain represents the largest component of our brain, and it is absolutely fascinating. Your delicate little (ok, big) subconscious is frightfully torn between two worlds: our prehistoric world and our current high-tech, always-on world.

Let's just take a minute to give our subconscious some recognition! It's apparently doing a hell of a job because you are still alive to read this book. However, by doing its job of keeping us alive, it is struggling to deal with prioritizing all of the insane inputs we are exposed to every hour of our day. So yes, it is incredible, but it is also at the root of our productivity issues.

Picture the subconscious as a tremendous big thirsty sponge. Every single piece of data coming in through our five senses is being sucked up by that sponge. Then it has the arduous task of deciding what data needs to be focused on by our conscious brain and what can just be stored away.

As a general rule, it is always going to focus on data that is perceived as a threat. Not unlike the bunny that forgot about its wonderful fresh grass, it was munching on when the coyote appeared. You may be hanging out on the couch, binge-watching Netflix, happy as a little clam. You are ignoring a million other things that are occurring. Until a robber bursts through your front door. So much for watching Netflix.

While Freud believed the unconscious/subconscious was inherently "bad," Carl Jung and modern practitioners, such as those that focus in the NLP discipline, believe it is not inherently evil and that you can work with the subconscious.

Think of a typical 7-year old child. Maybe you when you were a kid, perhaps your child, or a niece or nephew. When you are seven, you tend to take instructions very literally. You want to be "good," and you need clear directions.

Your subconscious brain is just like that 7-year old child. It is incredibly literal.

Here is a fundamental fact about the subconscious brain that plays a HUGE role in your productivity and general life fulfillment: it does not process negatives!

So let's say, for example, you are struggling paycheck-to-paycheck. If I asked you what your goal is, maybe you would respond, "I don't want to be broke anymore."

When the subconscious reads that message, that thought, it reads it as a positive. "Oh! You want to be broke! Ok! I've got you covered!" It continues to direct energy towards the state of being broke.

It seems a bit strange, doesn't it? But it is entirely accurate. People who think and talk about sickness are sicker. People who think and talk about being poor are more impoverished. People who think and talk about being prosperous are more prosperous. Later in this book, I am going to provide you with additional information on this, but it is crucial to understand this incredible and inseparable connection between our thoughts and our circumstances.

I challenge you to monitor your thoughts. Check yourself on how many times a day you are thinking in the negative. And when you find yourself thinking negatively, stop and immediately reframe the thought.

How often have you had these thoughts?

"I wish I wasn't fat / lazy / tired / broke / alone / ugly / old, etc."

"I can't get everything done."

"I am not appreciated at my job / at home / by my family / by my friends."

"I am not making progress against my goals."

"I'll never be able to afford that."

"I can't do that."

When we think and talk in the negative, our subconscious does not recognize that as an anti-state, instead, it aligns your energy with maintaining it, as if it was positive. We find ourselves taking action, subconsciously, in that direction, versus trying to reverse it.

We must practice taking every thought captive, and I would vehemently agree. Your thoughts become your words; your words become your actions; your actions define your life. Essentially our thoughts create a self-fulfilling prophecy. There is no denying the mind-body connection.

Stress

When the limbic system receives a stress input, the amygdala fires up and releases stress hormones. When the brain stem gets the message of the stress hormones, it will increase our respirations, change our blood flow, dilate our pupils, and increase our heart rate.

Like our brain stem, our subconscious loves homeostasis and perceives a change in our environment as a potential threat to our survival. Again, this is due to the core function of the survival of our species. If the limbic system was wallowing in happiness looking at a pretty blue sky, we might not notice the great big grizzly bear getting ready to eat us.

The subconscious brain actively seeks out and prioritizes negative situations.

What does the subconscious consider a negative situation? Absolutely anything that is a threat to homeostasis. Remember, our brain has one purpose: keep us alive. This is why change and disruptions are so impactful to our productivity. We are wired to respond to change as if it is terrible, even if it is a positive change.

Throughout this book and the nine-step process of GET IT DONE, you will be working on changing the way your subconscious interprets the inputs so that it does not see them as a threat. This is a necessary component of changing our behavior.

Our Memories

As mentioned, our subconscious brain receives input and impressions from our environment and determines what to do with that information. For just a minute, consider the millions of impressions that are being sent to your subconscious brain at this very moment. Your skin alone is transmitting a constant barrage of information. Think of all of the sounds you are hearing, everything you are seeing, tasting, and smelling.

Research estimates that the brain can only handle and process about 100 pieces of information every second. Your skin alone is made up of 20 square feet of nerve cells. Your eyes capture 300 megapixels of visual information every second. Thank goodness we have the subconscious brain and what is known as the reticular activating system (RAS) to control the flow. Just think how overwhelming this insane barrage would be for our conscious brain to handle.

Evert action, input, and interaction create an imprint. Those imprints create our memories. As memories are formed, the limbic system decides which of those should be short-term memories and those that should be filed away as long-term memories. These memories are stored in different regions of our brain.

They are finding that many people on the autism spectrum can easily access their long-term memories but are more challenged to access their short-term memories. This is the opposite of typical brain function.

But here is something else that happens with those memories: They are not only stored, but they are also tagged with an emotion: a happy memory, a sad memory, traumatic memory... Just as we may tag a blog post to create categories of topics, the limbic system tags our memories. As part of this process, you will be essentially reprogramming some of those tags to increase your choices and improve your results. Consider it therapy in a book!

The Conscious Brain

Now here is where it gets really good! As a human being, we have the benefit of a bonus section, beyond just the reptilian and mammalian brains. It is this part of the brain, the neocortex, that makes us different than our animal and reptile friends. Sometimes referred to as the "executive brain," this is where logic and rational thought are invoked. In this book, we will consider this our conscious brain. This conscious brain is a much smaller percentage of our brain than the subconscious.

The challenge that we face is that the primitive areas of our brain are stronger than our conscious brain. In situations of high stress, we may experience what is considered an "amygdala hijack," where the executive brain is left out of the communication loop. It is literally short-circuited and shut off. We go into autopilot during times of high stress.

Think of a time when you acted completely irrationally in a situation. Later, as you thought back to the situation, you realized just how ridiculous your actions had been. The most common example is road rage. We have all got those stories. Doh! "I can't believe I said that / did that / acted that way."

Here is the challenge. Your subconscious brain executes based on routines, is impulsive, and is driven by emotions. It is always on, and it processes information much faster than the conscious brain. Meanwhile, your conscious brain is voluntary and effortful. But much slower.

To improve your intelligent productivity, you will be engaging your conscious brain with your subconscious brain in a new manner, to override some of your primal instincts and align better with today's environment. This means that you will be increasing your neuroplasticity.

Neuroplasticity is the ability to create new neural pathways in our brain. Isn't that exciting? We can make more of them! More neural pathways mean an increase in our ability to intelligently process information, make decisions, and choose the best option. Throughout this book, I am going to be providing you with straight-forward techniques to increase your neuroplasticity.

So put the planner down and step away, slowly and carefully. Do not look at your to-do list. Forget all of those apps on your phone. We are working on understanding the why so that we can genuinely change our outcomes.

Our Need for Productivity

As a kid, I wanted to be a forensic pathologist, inspired by the show Quincy. But my life took some unexpected turns, and medical school was not a viable option. However, my interest in human pathology led me to an undergraduate and graduate focus on psychology.

I became obsessed with understanding human behavior: my own and others. Why did some people thrive in seemingly horrible conditions, while others went down a path of self-destruction in the most perfect of environments?

A primary driver of this obsession was that I did appear to be *different* than others. That fascinated me. Why was I different? If anything, I saw myself as having less potential than others (subconscious programming). I struggled (and still do) with imposter syndrome. Yet, people were asking *me* how I accomplished what I accomplished. I wanted to figure it out. I was curious about what made me tick.

A Quick Psych Lesson

During my undergrad, I studied many theorists. While I was intrigued by them all, it was Alfred Adler who specifically piqued my interest. Adler was a cohort of Sigmund Freud, but the two parted ways, somewhat pretentiously, when Adler presented a differing opinion from Freud's.

Adler established what was known as individual psychology. He believed that a person was not a product of their past, but rather a culmination of all of their experiences. The word individual, in individual psychology, literally means "unable to be divided." Adler believed that human beings strive for perfection and have a desire to fulfill their potential. Abraham Maslow would later call this the concept of "self-actualization."

One of the most compelling aspects of Adler's approach was his work within the Vienna prison system. While one group of repeat offenders was provided with traditional Freudian psychotherapy, a second group was also introduced to goal achievement therapy. Inmates set goals and worked to achieve those goals. As they succeeded, their confidence increased, and they continued to progress on a positive trajectory. The rates of reoffending were radically different from the goal-driven group.

What does this tell us about human behavior? When we have something to look forward to, we are more motivated by a clear picture of what we can accomplish. We also receive a beautiful hit of endorphins when we achieve our goals. More on this later!

Let's partner up the lessons from Adler with another famous psychotherapist: Viktor Frankl. Viktor Frankl was imprisoned in the Nazi concentration camps in the 1940s. Influenced by Adler's work, Frankl developed logotherapy. Frankl believed that individuals are motivated by a will to meaning, as so described in his book "Man's Search for Meaning."

I believe a large part of our productivity challenge stems from the fact that we struggle for meaning in our current lives. We are torn in a million directions, and to make matters worse, we live in a highly comparative society. Facebook, Instagram and other social media channels continually show us what we are *not*. It can be hard to find meaning in a job that does not leave you fulfilled or a life that is nothing more than constant stress.

Frankl also believed that the last of the human freedoms is our attitude. It is the only thing that cannot be taken from us. He drew on his experiences in the concentration camps. The prisoners were literally stripped of everything: their possessions, their families, their dignity, and even their identities, reduced to nothing but tattooed numbers.

This is my favorite quote from Frankl:

"Between stimulus and response, there is a space. In that space is our power to choose our response. In our response lies our growth and our freedom."

This concept of choosing our response will be explored as part of our GET IT DONE process. Carefully choosing your response is a hallmark of emotional intelligence. And it is a decision that you repeatedly make throughout your day.

Intelligent productivity is choosing the most appropriate response despite the stimulus.

Admit It. You Procrastinate.

In Latin, *cras* is tomorrow, and *crastinus* is belonging to tomorrow. Procrastination is the act of delaying or postponing something that we need to do.

Procrastination is a fundamental human condition, a result of subconscious patterning that is actually linked to our survival instinct. Observe children playing. They are having fun, laughing, and overflowing with creativity. And then you ask them to pick up their toys. Nearly all children, unless threatened with the fear of God (i.e., a coyote!), will dawdle, delay, and show less than an enthusiastic response.

If we have an option to do something fun versus do something challenging, tedious, or frustrating, of course, we will pick the fun activity. But as we mature, we get stuck in the middle of a tug-of-war. A big, ongoing tug-of-war.

Our neocortex rationalizes that life is not all play. Society, our family, our friends, and our own goals, put pressure on us to work, to do the un-fun stuff. Do laundry, pay bills, finish the report for work, complete our school assignments. These are our must-dos. And if you are like most people, they are not necessarily pleasurable. This is because we have programmed them within our subconscious as not fun.

But while we are pushing ourselves to do this un-fun stuff, we are tempted and distracted with anything and everything that is fun! Fabulous vacations, delicious dinners, exciting adventures. Thank you, social media, for showing me how my life is not as glamorous as others!

It is very typical human behavior to delay unpleasurable tasks until it gets to a critical point. This is known as student syndrome. Very few students (young and old, alike) will do an assignment until the due date is within a short window.

While this may seem like a bad thing, honestly, we tend to do better work when we have the appropriate amount of stress and tension to give us a nice hit of adrenaline. I am going to discuss how to leverage that tension in the GET IT DONE processes. We can use student syndrome as a valuable asset versus to our detriment.

Are You Ready?

The remainder of the book is a proven nine-step GET IT DONE program to revolutionize the way you operate on a daily basis.

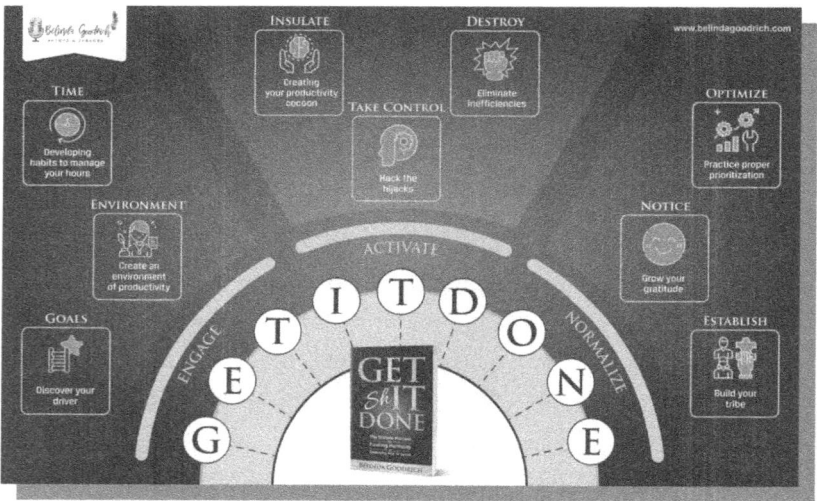

The nine steps are spread over three distinct areas:

In the first area, we will be working on a foundation to **ENGAGE** you, mind, and body, in the creation of your ideal work and life environment.

There will be three steps:

Step One: G – Goals

Step Two: E – Environment

Step Three: T – Time

In the second area, your foundation will be **ACTIVATED**. This will include taking action on new behaviors and conditioning. The three steps in activation will be:

Step Four: I – Insulate

Step Five: T – Take control

Step Six: D – Destroy

And finally, in the third area, we are going to **NORMALIZE** this behavior in a way that creates no other option but for you to be happy, fulfilled, and productive. Your relationship with your daily work has changed, and I am going to provide you with reinforcements so that you will be successful long term.

The three steps in normalizing will be:

Step Seven: O – Optimize

Step Eight: N – Notice

Step Nine: E – Establish

Let's GET IT DONE!

Belinda Goodrich

Section 1

ENGAGE

Steps 1 - 3

Belinda Goodrich

STEP 1: GOALS

DISCOVER YOUR DRIVER

The first step in your nine-step program to GET IT DONE is to define and be able to articulate your goals clearly. Consider the GPS in your car. You get in your car, ready to head out on a road trip to a particular destination. You don't merely acknowledge the GPS is there. You don't expect the GPS to read your mind. You must enter the destination. Otherwise, it is not going to do a damn thing for you.

Our Internal GPS

We all have an inner GPS. We are amazing, intelligent, and spiritual creatures. We are naturally pulled towards our "destinations." Yet so many of us never think actually to plug our desired destination into our internal GPS. We become an observer of our lives versus an active participant.

If you want to be more productive, happier, and fulfilled, you must define where you are going in all aspects of your life: work, home, family, friends, pursuits.

Picture this…

You arrive at the funeral home. As you walk in, the funeral director greets you and escorts you to the appropriate room. He is a proper man, but with gentle kindness. You stand at the back of the room, taking in the details of the gathering in front of you.

You look around and recognize people from your life: your family, your friends, your co-workers. You see that sweet girl that takes your order at the local coffee shop. The room is full of people that you have interacted with over your life.

You slowly make your way to the front and look down into the casket.

You see yourself.

You turn around and find a seat in the front row.

After a few moments, the attendees begin to come forward, one at a time, to speak.

Carefully consider this. What are they saying about you? How do their words make you feel? Are their words consistent, or do different groups describe you as though you were utterly separate people?

A macabre exercise? Perhaps.

But, my friend, it is a reality. We are all going to die. It is truly the only certainty in life. The day will come where people that were in your life will come to mourn your death and celebrate your life.

Will they say you were harried, stressed, frustrated, exhausted, unhappy, unfulfilled? Or will they say that you were living your best life? That you had a clear mission, and you lived out that mission every day? That you were happy, fulfilled, and when you walked in the room, the room lit up with your awesomeness?

What story will they tell? How many people are you affecting, and how are you affecting them?

Every moment of every day, we have a choice about how we are affecting those around us. It is a choice — a powerful one and one that you own.

This is precisely why the first step to getting shit done is to align the shit we are doing with the shit that we should be doing to live that glorious life that will live on after our days on this earth are gone.

Here is my first big piece of advice:

Stop wasting your time on stupid shit that doesn't matter and

doesn't lend to that amazing life that you want! Just STOP it.

So ask yourself these questions:

Why am I here?

What is my purpose?

What do I want my legacy to be long after I'm gone?

And lastly...

What am I doing right now to live my purpose and my legacy?

As Viktor Frankl reminded us, we are beings searching for meaning in our lives. The first step in improving your productivity is not merely just doing more work and being busier, but it is genuinely identifying what you should *actually* be doing.

What you do with your waking hours needs to reflect your mission in life. Nothing more. Nothing less. Every moment of every day. Every choice you make.

I was at a National Speakers Association (NSA) meeting when I heard something compelling. Something so powerful, that it changed the way I viewed every action I took.

The message was simple:

"How would the person I want to be, behave, act, and focus their time? Would the person I want to be, be doing the things I'm doing right now?"

Take a minute to think about your day, your week, your month. Is the activity and energy you've used been entirely in alignment with the person you want to be? All of the time? Most of the time? Some of the time? None of the time?

Let's say you want to be a best-selling author. Would a best-selling author be sitting at their desk scrolling through Facebook? Or would they be writing manuscripts, learning their craft, creating material?

This was a major reality check for me. I realized that there was an incongruency between what I dreamed of being and the person that I was currently – in action and energy. Was I ever going to be the person I dreamed about being doing things that did not support that dream? Absolutely not.

And now, it's a question I ask myself throughout the day. It keeps me in check and reminds me of what I should be doing. I take it so seriously that I hold myself accountable not only in my thoughts but in my words, as well.

I start each morning writing in my journal. I recap the day prior and set my goals and intentions for the day before me. This is NOT a to-do list. This is a written statement of how I will choose to live my life that day, including the key things that I will focus on during the coming hours.

The last thing I do before going to sleep is a retrospective of my day. What went well, what did not go well, what do I want to change tomorrow? I practice gratitude by writing down the fantastic things that happened.

We must keep our attention and focus on what it is we want with this all-to-brief life of ours.

Think of it this way: you plug your destination into your GPS while standing in your living room. You set it down. Leave your house and get in your car, intent on getting to that destination. How effective is that GPS going to be if it's hanging out in your living room and you are out in your car? It's not! We have to keep our GPS with us at all times!

There's a joke about a man who prays to God to win the lottery. Week after week goes by, and the man does not win. He gets angry and frustrated with God. Finally, God says to him, "my child, to win the lottery, you must first buy a ticket!"

If we have a desire to create a better life, yet do not take deliberate action to enable that better life to happen, we are no better than the man who wanted to win the lottery but did not buy a ticket.

It is time to think about *your* life. What is most important to you?

Life Inventory Exercise

Consider each of the following dimensions of your life. On a scale of 1 to 10, score yourself against each dimension: 1 extremely dissatisfied to 10 extremely satisfied.

SCORE	DIMENSION
	My spiritual life (religious or other-dimensional)
	My self-image
	My career or profession
	My financial well-being
	My health
	My family
	My friendships and relationships
	My community
	My romantic relationship
	My fun pursuits and recreation
	My contribution to society and the greater good
	My personal growth

What do those scores reveal about you and your current satisfaction with your life and pursuits? Have these dynamics changed over the years? Have you become more or less satisfied with different areas?

What has improved over the last three years, and why?

_____

_____

_____

_____

_____

What has deteriorated over the last three years, and why?

_____

_____

_____

_____

_____

What is the one area that you are most negatively affected by? Why?

_____

_____

_____

_____

This can be a tough exercise, so give yourself a little bit of grace on it. People tend to act in a bit of pendulum fashion: whatever is bothering them the most (or giving them the most pleasure), they will apply the majority of their focus. In doing so, the other areas will suffer.

Let's say you've gained weight recently, and it is making you very uncomfortable. You commit to an exercise routine and start seeing results. You are so motivated that you prioritize exercising over time with your family and friends.

Gradually those relationships begin to erode a bit. Maybe your partner is jealous of the time you are spending away from them, or your kids tell you you're not attentive.

So, you back off your exercise routine and begin to gain weight. Back and forth. Back and forth.

We need to stop the pendulum. Or at the very least make the swing of the pendulum not so dramatic.

I will challenge you that when you can more closely tune-in to your internal GPS, it will be easier to recognize any deviations and course-correct before things get to an extreme position.

Now that you have a proper assessment of where you are currently, let's take it up to a higher level and determine your life mission.

Your Life Mission Exercise

Consider your ideal life. Create a list of 20 things that you want to have, things you want to do, and things you want to be in that ideal life. Dig deep and be honest!

1 _____

2 _____

3 _____

4 _____

5 _____

6 _____

7 _____

8 _____

9 _____

10 _____

11 _____

12 _____

13 _____

14 _____

15 _____

16 _____

17 _____

18 _____

19 _____

20 _____

Consider your list. What is the absolute most crucial thing on the list, if you could only have one? Circle that one.

What is the second most important? Third? Fourth? Fifth? Label them as such. Using this information, you can now create your personal mission statement.

Our Measuring Stick

In project management, we create three baselines for our projects: one for the scope (work) of our project, one for the schedule (the time we have allocated to the project activities), and one for the cost (the money that we will spend). These performance measurement baselines are critical to the success of the project as they provide a measuring stick for our progress.

In comparing our actual progress to our baselines, we can identify any variances early and take the appropriate actions to bring the project back into alignment with those baselines. They give us compelling insight and data that not only improves the end-result, but they also allow us to collect meaningful data about what is working and what is not.

Without baselines, we would have no way of understanding our project progress. The same is true for your life. After all, your life is the most significant project you will ever have.

Your personal mission statement is your project management baseline! If you have no idea where you are going and what it is going to look like, how do you know what to do? If you don't have targets and a measuring stick, how do you know if you are doing well or doing poorly? You're essentially just floundering around like a cute little amoeba with no aim or direction.

Creating your personal mission statement gives you a ruler by which to measure every action you take and is the compass that defines the direction you should be moving in and towards.

Consider some of these personal mission statements:

Walt Disney's personal mission was "to make people happy."

Maya Angelou's was, "My mission in life is not merely to survive, but to thrive; and to do so with some passion, some compassion, some humor, and some style."

To craft your personal mission statement, answer the following questions:

1. What do you want your legacy to be?

2. Close your eyes and picture your ideal life. What do you see? What do you hear? What do you feel? What are you doing?

3. Go back to your funeral. How would the people closest to you describe you? Is that how you would like them to describe you?

Write your personal mission statement:

_____

_____

_____

_____

_____

_____

Now that you know your mission, your "why," the next step is to create a picture of what that looks like. In Napoleon Hill's best-selling book Think & Grow Rich, he exclaims, "Whatever the mind of man can conceive and believe it can achieve!".

That visualization is so incredibly powerful. When the brain can see and visualize these images, it recognizes them as reality, and your energy starts to align around making them a reality. The doubt of achievement does not come from our brain; it sees the vision as reality. The uncertainty comes in through a flawed inner voice that has been programmed by your life experiences.

The Power of Visualization

Create a visual of your mission statement and the life that aligns with that mission statement. Keep it prominently displayed, such as in a vision board, a screen saver, a drawing. Anything that can trigger your brain to see it as a reality.

As my speaking and consulting business grew, I was finding myself on the road more and more. Realistically, it was not practical for me to have a large home with a yard that I would have to maintain. I knew that at that particular point in my life, less was more. What would better suit me to free up my time to activities that were priority would be to have a smaller place and no yard.

While considering where I would live, I moved into an apartment complex. Can I say that I am way too old to live in an apartment complex with a bunch of young people that like to party at night? I am an early morning person that works from home!

While I liked the "no maintenance" aspect of it, and I loved the location, I knew it was not a long-term solution. I found a condominium complex that was being built nearby. Occupied mainly with retirees, snowbirds, and professionals, the complex was quiet and with wonderful amenities. Looking at the floor plans, I knew this was where I needed to be.

The condo became my reality. I had a picture of the complex as the background on my laptop. I had a countdown clock on my phone that would tell me each day remaining until my unit would be ready. Free time was spent perusing paint and fabric swatches, picking out furniture, and creating a complete visual representation of my condo in my mind. I saw myself sitting at my desk in that home office writing books.

Here's the thing: I was self-employed and securing the mortgage for the condo was not a slam-dunk, done deal. If anything, the odds were stacked against me for several reasons. But every time that doubt would bubble up, I'd pop those damn bubbles. I'd look at the pictures; I'd feel the excitement around the countdown clock, I'd visualize parking my car in the garage and working in my office.

I'd check in with myself frequently. Were the actions that I was taking getting me closer to, or further away from my condo? My condo became my true north.

And today? I am writing this book while sitting in my beautiful condo, just as I visualized. Do not underestimate the power of positive visualization!

In the article 'Seeing is Believing: The Power of Visualization," published in 2009 by Psychology Today, the incredible effects of visualization are discussed. Natan Sharansky was a prisoner in the USSR for nine years after being accused of spying for the United States. During his time in solitary confinement, he played a mental game of chess, focusing on becoming the world champion. In 1996, Sharansky did precisely that by beating world champion chess player Garry Kasparov.

According to the article, research has demonstrated that "mental practices are almost effective as a true physical practice, and that doing both is more effective than either alone."

Jack Niklaus would create a vivid visualization before hitting any shot, even in practice. Boxing legend Muhammed Ali employed many different visualization techniques, including his affirmation, "I am the greatest!".

Another research study evaluated two groups of individuals that were seeking jobs. The first group was provided with typical interview coaching and career counseling. The second group was provided with interview coaching, career counseling, as well as teaching on visualization. Twenty-one percent of the first group was offered a job as compared to 66% of the second group.

When we make the unknown, known it helps us overcome fear and self-doubt.

The object of our focus determines our perception of reality.

For as long as she could remember, Stacie wanted to be a marine biologist. She loved all of the outdoors and nature, but her heart always pulled her to the coast and the amazing animals of the sea. Growing up in Maine, she would find herself at the beach, staring out at the ocean, imagining the whales, dolphins, and other creatures living beneath the surface.

Throughout school, Stacie did well. But not quite well enough to earn scholarships to college. While her family supported her dream of being a marine biologist, financially, that is all it would be: a dream. Stacie worked through high school at the local bank, and after she graduated, she was offered positions of progressive responsibility.

Every once in a while, feet in the sand at the beach, she would think about that dream of being more than a bank teller. She would think about swimming with dolphins, learning how to care for and protect them. But she accepted that it just wasn't to be. After all, she was now in her mid-twenties, a car payment, rent, and gas weren't cheap. She did not see how pursuing a degree was feasible.

One night, her friend invited her to a vision board party. It seemed a bit silly and juvenile to Stacie.

"So let me get this straight," she said "we sit around and cut pictures out of magazines and glue them to a poster board? It sounds very preschool-ish." But she needed a night out and maybe arts and crafts time would be a fun distraction from her relatively uneventful life.

As she sat there with a group of women drinking wine, listening to music, she considered the pile of magazines in the center of the table. "What should I be looking for?" she asked her friend. "What moves your soul? What catches your eye? What makes you smile? Pick those!"

Before long, Stacie's board was revealing a beautiful underwater world of fish, coral reefs, and dolphins; serene beaches, boats on the water. She also clipped a picture of a university with a marine biology program. Stepping back and considering what she had made, she realized it was her dream life.

With her vision board in her line of sight every day, she took a leap of faith and applied for admission to that school. Not only did she get accepted, but she was also able to use a combination of work-study, scholarships, and a part-time job to make it work financially. Every step she took was in direct alignment with the picture of her dream life.

The power of visualization is not some crazy type of black magic. Instead, it is ruminating on what you want, recognizing that the power comes from within, and then aligning your actions towards that desired reality. It's not abracadabra, hocus-pocus, a magic wand that is suddenly going to invoke the university to come knocking on your door.

As Genevieve Davis says in her book Becoming Magic, "The world does not respond to the waving of the wand, but *to the person doing the waving… the Magic itself always comes from the person doing the spell.*"

Stacie didn't run anxiously to the mailbox each day, expecting an engraved invitation to attend the university on a full-ride scholarship without even receiving her application. She simply evaluated every step she was taking in her life as getting her closer to or further away from her goal and modified her behavior accordingly.

Your Precious Internal GPS

Each of us has an incredible internal navigation program, guiding us to reconcile our actions with our dreams and goals.

Consider a very young baby. She spies a toy in front of her. She wants to touch, hold, and taste that toy. But this sweet little gal has not quite figured out how to make her hands and body move in a coordinated fashion to reach out and grab the toy.

Keeping her eyes fixed on the toy, her hand begins to make movements:

Too far left

Too far right

Ouch, she hit her face

Nope, that's her leg

Try, try, try, try.

With each movement, she recalibrates. She does not think to herself, "well, I'm just a dismal failure, a steaming pile of dog crap." No, not at all. She takes every movement in as feedback and then adjusts her next movement accordingly. She listens to her internal navigation program. There is no bad or wrong; she is just closer or further away from what she wants. That is it.

But then she grew up. She listened to big people. She watched other kids. She lost track of the utterly fantastic GPS rolling around inside of her. She could not quite define what *she* wanted versus what everyone was telling her she wanted.

The only thing that remained was emotions: positive emotions and negative emotions.

When she did things that aligned with her inner GPS, she felt happy emotions. When she deviated, she felt sad emotions. Eventually, she just chalked up those sad emotions to the realities of life.

The facts of life that are not real, but are rather the product of incorrect programming, such as:

- Life is hard
- Life sucks
- Being a grown-up isn't fun
- If you're having fun, you're not taking things seriously enough
- Work is called work for a reason
- Ugh, nobody likes Mondays

Antonio Damasio, a neuroscientist, uses the term *somatic marker* to describe that inner sensation we have attached to negative or positive emotion. We need to go back to our pre-societal programming days and get back in touch with those somatic markers. They give us data about our progress, allowing us to take control and make conscious choices to align more closely with our ideal life.

Somatic Markers

While I may not have had the best experiences in romantic relationships, I won the relationship lottery when it comes to my best friend. Ours is a friendship that grew slowly over time, beginning when we were just five years old. Like a fine wine, it has only gotten better with age.

Kim attended my mother's childcare center. Quiet, sweet, and unassuming, she was the perfect balance to my ever-present anxiousness. Being from a small town, we attended school together from kindergarten through graduation. In high school, quiet Kim became life-of-the-party Kim! Her bubbly confidence was, again, a perfect balance to my uncomfortable teenage awkwardness.

And so the story goes: through children, marriages, births, deaths, personal victories and tragedies our relationship grew, especially when we were able to sneak away from the chaos of life on a treasured girls' trip.

It was on a few of these recent trips that we discovered our "perfect happiness" – the Zen moment when everything feels right internally despite the chaos and turbulence of our lives.

One such moment occurred when we were sitting outside of a small, rustic camp in Maine, looking out over the lake, sipping a cold beverage, and appreciating the beautiful colors of the sunset. We both experienced pure bliss, pure joy, pure happiness. We were at peace. We were content. So much so, that we commented on it as such to each other, at the same time!

It was this unbelievable feeling of "oh, this is what life is supposed to feel like!".

Were our lives perfect? Quite the contrary. I had suffered some setbacks in my business, had recently lost my stepfather, and my mother's illness had become increasingly worse. Kim was facing the impending death of her only sister from an aggressive form of ALS, diagnosed just a few short months prior. She had given up her home and her job to care for her sister. Finances, family, and obligations weighed us both down.

In some ways, our lives were a mess. And yet, here we were basking in perceptible perfection.

This was our internal guidance system validating that we were in the right place at the right time doing the right thing.

It was so powerful that I took inventory of everything that made me feel that state of bliss. We were near the water, in nature, in our beloved home state. Our cell phones were off. No laptops. We were sitting quietly next to someone who we loved unconditionally and who loved us unconditionally.

We would revisit that same feeling of nirvana just three months later, sitting on the banks of the Seine in Paris.

Two months earlier, a month after that moment at camp, Kim's sister lost the battle against ALS. Ten days later, on the day of her sister's funeral, my mother passed away. We were both lost, hurt, and grieving but opted to go on my milestone birthday trip to my favorite city.

And there it was, on the last night in the City of Lights, we sat in silence. We had just enjoyed a nice dinner and river cruise. Sipping our wine, we took in the lights, basked in the perfect autumn temperatures, and enjoyed the sounds of the French language as lovers strolled by.

"I am completely and perfectly happy," I said. "Yes," she responded, "I was just thinking that very same thing.".

If you take nothing else away from this book, my friend, learn to listen to the beautiful inner voice. It will not steer you wrong. Seek out those positive emotions. Move away from those things that bring negative emotions. Step away from the conditioning of your past and step into the life that you so richly deserve.

But Work Sucks

I know what you're thinking. "But Belinda, if I move away from negative feelings, I'll never go back to work!".

Are you indeed that unhappy at work? Versus quitting your job, evaluate what exactly about it is making you miserable. Is it the job itself? Is it the people? Is it the hours? The location?

Now consider all of those things that you have and do as a result of your job. Do they bring you joy? Is the joy greater than the pain? What are some actions you could take to make the pain less and the joy more?

And ultimately, listen to your navigation.

I like to say that I was born without a filter. Even if I could control what comes out of my mouth, my face would give everything away. I will never, ever be a poker champion. You never have to guess what I am thinking. My face will tell you everything!

When I first started in corporate America, I did not fully appreciate the fact that employees were expected to have a highly functioning filter. I had been raised by parents that owned their business, I owned my own business, and to me, if something wasn't 'right,' you said something.

After being reprimanded a few times for speaking out, I started to be programmed not to respond. Essentially, I was being trained to go against my internal GPS. Those times when I couldn't help myself but speak out, I would affectionately coin "career-limiting moves (CLMs)." I had several CLMs.

But after staying quiet during one particularly unethical situation, I vowed that I would never do so again. This was a tough commitment to live up to, though. I was a single mother, raising three children, living paycheck-to-paycheck, and they were counting on me to support them.

But I went bigger than that. In my life's mission statement, I say I will do right and will not tolerate wrong. I wanted my girls to grow up to have a voice and to use their voices. Ultimately, I wanted them to respect me. At my funeral, I want people to say she lived her mission, despite the potential personal cost.

How did I know when I should take a CLM? It was that feeling. That intuition and pull deep down inside my belly. The negative feeling that pressed against my lungs, making it difficult to breathe. I started listening to it.

And here's the crazy thing that happened. My CLMs did not limit my career, it *flourished*.

In the ultimate CLM example, I had a life-defining moment while I was in India. I realized that my work was not aligning with my beliefs. Sure, I had a great salary, excellent benefits, and an executive title. But what I did not have was the opportunity to use what I believed were my strengths and passions: my gifts. It wasn't long after my return from India that I quit my job to start my own business. One that did fully align with those gifts and my mission statement. And despite the ups and downs, I have never once regretted that decision.

Listen to your navigation!

Habit #1: Tune in frequently to your internal guidance system: your intuition, your emotions, your gut. And always trust it.

Key Take-Aways From Step One

1. Take time to consider how you want to live your life and how you want to be remembered

2. Your goals and personal mission statement become your GPS

3. Visualization is the most powerful step in creating the ideal life

4. Listen to the emotions that are coming from your internal voice, your navigation system

Belinda Goodrich

ENVIRONMENT

Create an
environment
of productivity

STEP 2: ENVIRONMENT

*CREATE AN ENVIRONMENT OF
PRODUCTIVITY – INTERNALLY AND
EXTERNALLY!*

In Step One, you created your life mission statement and identified your true north. The next step is evaluating the environment in which you are achieving those goals and living out your life mission.

One of the biggest challenges that we face in being productive is our environment. We are inundated with both sensory and emotional distractions every nanosecond. Your environment needs to be as interruption-free as humanly possible. (I know, that's pretty laughable in today's world, right?) With the average attention span approximately 8 seconds, it does not take much for something shiny to catch our eye and pull us away from something more appropriate.

Attention deficit hyperactivity disorder (ADHD) is considered a neuro*atypical* condition, often linked and related to other disorders on the autism spectrum: autism, dyslexia, Asperger's, anxiety, etc. It is estimated that approximately 30% of the workforce will be neuroatypical within the next five years. While there is research being conducted that has yet to yield any definitive answers, the cause of these neuroatypical conditions appears to be somewhat of a mystery.

It is likely that, in many cases, there is an underlying medical cause, but I believe that we are also susceptible from an environmental perspective, in two ways.

First, consider our environments today versus how they were even 20 short years ago. If we wanted to talk to someone who was not in our immediate environment, we had the option of finding a phone, dialing their number (which we either had memorized or looked up in a phone book), or mailing them a letter.

There was no instantaneous conversation with someone else located anywhere in the world. No texts, no instant messages, no likes or comments on our social media pages, no FaceTime or video calls. To engage in communication, it took thought, and it took time. Today, we press a button.

And it's not just the always-on communication; it is the fact that there are so *many* communication vehicles. Think about sitting down at your desk to start working. Each time you receive an email, a pop-up notification appears usually associated with a "ding." Ding! Ding!

Your internet browsers are open. Someone commented on your Facebook post: Ding! You received a reply to a message on LinkedIn: Ding! Someone sent you a Snap Chat: Ding!

Ding! Ding! Ding! Ding!

And we think that Attention Deficit is simply a medical condition? Could it be that we cannot focus because there are way too many real-time stimuli?

Here is another aspect to consider: not only do we have an environment of distractions, but we are also programming ourselves to expect and react to those distractions.

Think about it this way. Have you ever been going about your business, and you realize "hmmmm... things are awfully quiet. Why haven't I received any texts / emails / Facebook notifications / Snapchats in a while?" So you look at your phone or computer to see *what is wrong*. Because, of course, something must be wrong! Things are *too quiet!* So even when the vehicles are not distracting us, the lack of vehicles is also distracting us!

Remember, our brain is relatively simple. It LOVES homeostasis.

If you are living and breathing and surviving in your current state, your mind is happy. It is hardwired to do one job. Keep you alive. Every DING! represents a potential change. And in your brain's world, it perceived a change as a threat to homeostasis, so we better check it out and assess that threat. Or, the opposite has occurred, and we have become so assimilated to the DINGs that now we have to divert our attention when we haven't had any recently!

To think that we can block out the DING! is somewhat unrealistic.

Unless...

When was the last time you were engrossed in a TV show, an activity, a conversation? You were all in – gangbusters! Before you knew it, an hour had gone by, and just maybe during that time, you did not think to check social media or look at your phone.

So, I challenge the thought that we have an 8-second attention span. I would be more likely to agree that we allow ourselves to get distracted every eight seconds. What we have to do is create the environment and tasks to keep us focused, train our brain to move away from the constant shifting.

Let's break down all of the various distractions that we encounter. Generally speaking, there are two categories of distractions: sensory and emotional.

Sensory Distractions

As discussed at the start of this chapter, sensory distractions are being lobbed at us consistently and continuously, 24 hours per day, through our five basic senses:

- Visual – what we see
- Auditory – what we hear
- Kinesthetic – what we feel
- Olfactory – what we smell
- Gustatory – what we taste

Consider your environment right now as you read this book. You see or maybe hear the words; you feel the book or the device in your hand or maybe headphones in your ears. But consider beyond this book. What other sensory distractions are you experiencing?

- The loud guy in the cubical next to you
- The taste of peppermint gum in your mouth
- The air conditioning blasting on high to the point that you can't feel your toes
- A throbbing toe that you just stubbed
- The sun streaming through the window
- The smell of someone cooking fish in the microwave in the lunchroom (C'mon guys! Social etiquette here – do not cook fish in the microwave in a public place!)

As you are being flooded with all of these sensory distractions, your brain is efficiently and methodically determining what needs your attention, a continuous effort of prioritization.

Consider the temperature in the room. Personally, for me, despite being a 5th generation Mainer, I hate being cold (thus the reason I moved to Arizona!). A comfortable temperature for me when I'm working at my computer is about 74°, I may not notice when the heat increases to 75°, but at 76° suddenly, my brain sends me a disruptive message to say, "you're hot, take action." Vice versa, the room cooling to 73° may not warrant a response, but at 71° or 72°, my body begins to shiver, and my brain interrupts whatever my priority is at that moment, letting me know I'm cold.

This was a big productivity challenge for me when I worked in a corporate environment. The offices were kept so cold that I was always shivering, and my hands would cramp while trying to work on my computer. I was miserable. This then kicked off a negative feedback cycle. The colder I felt, the more distracted I became. I attached negative emotion to the fact that I was cold, which then created an entire feeling of general negativity around me. And then, Belinda was cranky. Yes, I was that employee that got busted with a space heater under my desk!

With my office at home, I have very purposely created my nest of productivity that compliments all of my senses:

- Visual: I have big windows on either side of me so that I can see sunlight, rain, sunrises, sunsets, hummingbirds at the feeder. These windows are in my peripheral vision, not distracting me, but creating a soothing environment. On the wall directly in front of me, I have books from the floor to the ceiling. I am a major bibliophile, and just seeing books makes me happy. Between the rows of books are pictures of my family. Just a simple glance up and beyond my monitor are the things that I love the most in this world. My walls are painted a combination of a soothing light blue and a warm beige. The rug is gray, with sheer curtains hanging at the window.

- Auditory: I cannot function in complete silence. It just does not work for me. My go-to is country music, played at just the right volume to create a background ambiance without interrupting or disrupting my thought patterns. Because the majority of the music is songs that I know, I do not have to strain to pay attention to them. My brain does not register them as a threat to my homeostasis; instead, it accepts them as a comfortable known.

- Kinesthetic: I cannot underscore the importance of a good chair and desk set-up, being aware of ergonomics. I spend a lot of time on my computer. I need to be comfortable. Think about your keyboard, your mouse, your chair. Also, consider the temperature and temperature fluctuations. As I mentioned above, I am sensitive to the temperature in my office, so that stays pretty constant.

- Olfactory: Over the years, I have recognized how impactful scents can be to my productivity. Depending on the time of day or the type of work I'm doing, I may burn a candle with a comforting scent or use my diffuser with some essential oils. My go-to essential oils for focus: peppermint, orange, lemon, and rosemary. When I want to relax, I use lavender. Again, this was a challenge for me in the corporate setting when I'd have that co-worker that opted to bathe in an unappealing perfume or cologne. So much so, that there were a few times that I had to confront the offender, as nicely as possible, of course!

- Gustatory: A positive side-effect of living in Arizona is that I drink a lot of water (great for thinking, creating, and general health). Occasionally, I want a little more taste, so I'll grab flavored sparkling water, tea, or put some fruit in my water. Years ago, I broke myself of a 2-liter per day dependency on Diet Coke. I find the flavored sparkling waters a great alternative. If I have a snacking weakness when I'm working, it's mints: giving me both the gustatory and olfactory pep!

As you evaluate your environment, consider how to balance your sensory distractions to place you in the most advantageous position for productivity. You have to recognize that everyone is different; everyone is unique. And even day-to-day, your preferences may vary depending on your mood and the type of work you're doing.

If you are in a corporate setting or shared workspace, you may have to make some modifications to be respectful to those around you: music through headphones, a sweater if you're cold (not a space heater!), dabbing essential oils on your wrist versus in a diffuser.

Do not underestimate taking steps to create the ideal environment. You need your brainpower on the work that needs to be done, not festering negativity over being uncomfortable.

Create Your Ideal Environment Exercise:

Take a few minutes to visualize your ideal environment. Close your eyes, focusing on your breath, and clearing your mind. Imagine that you are being escorted to an empty room. It is a blank canvas, and you have the power to design it any way that you see fit.

First, consider what you want to see: what color are the walls? The carpet or flooring? Do you have windows and/or doors? What is the view outside of those windows or doors? Do you have pictures in your workspace? Who or what is in those pictures? What about motivational or inspirational posters? Awards, certificates, other accomplishments? Do you favor a Joanna Gaines' style, or are you more comfortable with sleek, modern fixtures?

Next, think about what sounds may be comforting, energizing, or motivating. Maybe it's music, or perhaps it's just white noise. Or maybe you want absolute silence. Do you prefer to hear other people talking and working in the background?

Now think about your chair, desk, and workspace. What does it feel like? What is the temperature in the room that would allow you to be most productive and least distracted?

Take a deep breath.

Imagine what your productivity haven smells like. Is there a smell or scent that relaxes you, motivates you, stimulates your creativity?

And lastly, consider tastes. What flavor do you prefer, if any? Do you want to be sipping cold water or hot tea? Chewing gum? Enjoying a nice chilled glass of chardonnay? (Ok, scratch that last one, it's typically not socially acceptable at work!)

Take another deep breath and look around the room that you have now visualized. Now consider the sound, the feel, the smell, and the taste. Freeze that room in your mind. Freeze the feeling of productivity, wellness, focus, and balance that you have associated with that room.

As you approach your work, your life, your focused time, do your best to recreate that state and that feeling. How can you incorporate some of what you just visualized in your day-to-day environment?

Habit #2: Consistently evaluate your physical environment to make adjustments in alignment with your preferred sensory inputs.

Emotional Distractions

The more disruptive and damaging distractions are emotional distractions. Picture that you are in the local coffee shop, bustling with the comings and goings of folks. Despite the background noise of the conversations, you can stay focused on the report that is due tomorrow.

But then suddenly you hear your name. Regardless of the priority of the report, you are going to give your attention to determining who said your name. This is considered an emotional distraction. Why did they say your name? What does it mean? Do you know them?

Emotional distractions have the power to completely derail your progress, your focus, and your priorities.

Alicia was a high-performing director for a progressive marketing firm. A dedicated and driven professional, she appeared to always be in control. Until the day she wasn't. She received a call from her adult daughter, Emily:

"Good morning, honey. I'm just walking into my office. What's up?" she answered hurriedly, giving the clear message that work was the priority.

"Mom, I need to tell you something. It's important." was the timid response.

Alicia immediately sensed that this was serious and closed her office door; her heart began beating faster.

"I'm pregnant," her daughter whispered, barely audible. Alicia could hear the emotion in her daughter's voice as she fought tears.

"Oh, honey, it's ok! Everything will be ok. We love you, and we are here to support you and this baby." While the timing was certainly not ideal, Alicia kicked into problem-solving mode. She had faith in her daughter and knew that Emily would be fine. The road ahead would be tough, but she vowed to help her daughter in any way that was needed.

"No, Mom," her daughter responded forcefully. "I'm not keeping it. My boyfriend is bringing me to the clinic this afternoon to terminate the pregnancy."

Alicia was stunned and saddened. It seemed to be such a dramatic and rash response. She loved her daughter more than anything, and the moment she was told of the pregnancy, she loved that grandchild. She was at once broken up emotionally not only over the loss of the grandchild but the agony of what her child was about to face and grow through.

As her daughter hung up, not allowing any further discussion, a knock at the door startled Alicia.

"Are you ready? It's time for your board presentation." It was her boss, Gerald, looking at her with a quizzical expression. In all of his years in working with her, he had never seen her ruffled, let alone in a state of evident dismay and overwhelm.

"Um.... no, Gerald. I just can't." the words were barely a whisper.

"What's going on, Alicia?" he asked. 'I just can't' was not an acceptable response. But looking at her ashen complexion and the tears welling in her eyes, he knew something was very wrong.

"It's a family situation with Emily."

"Oh no, is she ok?" based on her reaction, he feared the worst.

"I, I just don't know. But yes, she's ok, physically. Kind of."

Regardless of the situation, Gerald quickly realized that Alicia was in no condition to go in front of the board. He assured her that he was here if she wanted to talk and let her know that he would reschedule the meeting.

Alicia's situation may seem extreme. However, when we are dealing with emotional distractions, real or even perceived, it blocks us from engaging with our other responsibilities.

There was a time, not very long ago, when people were expected to block their emotions and leave any drama at the door of the workplace. But we are complex beings, and it is not that easy.

As I have mentioned previously, we cannot multitask effectively, even if that multitasking is in the form of splitting our attention between work that needs to be done and the emotional distraction that is weighing us down.

This is where you may be thinking that herein lies the benefit of compartmentalizing. You know, when you stuff something down deep in a box, close the lid, and put a big fat lock on it. I hate to tell you this, but compartmentalization is NOT a good option... You see, when you place your crap in a box, it does not go away. Regardless of how big the lock is. That crap begins to ooze out, whether you like it or not.

That ooze creates nasty, bitter seeds. Those seeds grow vile weeds. And those weeds eventually choke out your ability to function with love and humanity.

Dig that shit out. Do not let it fester. You may think you have it all under control, but I am here to tell you that you do not.

Having said that, however, there is a difference between dwelling on something negative and working at finding a resolution to the situation. When I say dig it out, that does not mean that you are going to sit there stewing about how you were violated, how you are a victim, or how the world is doing you wrong. Absolutely not!

It means dig it up and lay it out in front of you. Inspect it and analyze it. Find the why behind the situation, the seeds, and the bitterness. Most likely, it is either a communication issue or a lack of empathy for the other person or people involved in the situation. Or maybe you are just merely falling into victim mode, festering an extrinsic locus of control – meaning it is happening *to you*.

Albert Einstein is credited with saying, "we cannot solve our problems with the same level of thinking that created them." So go beyond. And deal with it to eliminate it.

Dealing with Emotional Distractions

Process for dealing with emotional distractions:

- **Verbally (yes, out loud) state the emotion you are feeling about the situation.** For example, maybe you are feeling hurt or angry. Say it out loud: "I feel hurt." This reframing technique breaks the emotional hold and amygdala hijack that you have going on, inviting your neocortex to come to the party. When the neocortex gets involved, you begin to engage in rational thought about the situation.

- **Look at the situation as an observer, not as a participant.** As soon as you re-live the situation as a participant, your emotional centers are going to go crazy again. Remember that our brain does not distinguish between reality and memory when it comes to emotions. If you simply re-live it, the neocortex is going to get uninvited to the pity party your holding, and you are going to be back in that overreaction mode.

- **Take the role of the opposing party or parties.** I know that's a tough one. But walk through the situation as if you were in their shoes. Try to think as they think, not as you perceive them to be. Assume positive intent.

- **Take ownership of your feelings and behaviors.** Could you have handled the situation differently? If you had an opportunity to have the situation occur again, how would you handle it in retrospect? Reach up into that big, beautiful brain of yours and imagine hitting a button to mute your irrational emotions. You are only left with rational thought. Does the situation look different?

- **Now it is time to make a decision.** Can you resolve the situation, or is it something that is, as you perceive it, impossible to resolve? If resolution is probable, brainstorm the actual steps you can take to solve the problem.

Often it may be as simple as picking up the phone and talking to the person, perhaps offering an apology for your role in the conflict.

If it is impossible to resolve the conflict, in the words of Elsa, "let it go!". Do not dwell on it. Do not revisit it. Do not tell other people about it. Do not vent. Do not bitch. Do not carry that big ass chip on your shoulder. Let. It. Go. If it is unresolvable, you carrying it with you is only weighing you down without doing anything to change the situation.

Daniel Goleman, in his book Focus, puts it this way: "Failure to drop one focus and move on to others can, for example, leave the mind lost in repeating loops of chronic anxiety."

Dealing with sensory distractions is relatively easy, but emotional distractions are much more challenging. And much more damaging.

Habit #3: Practice conducting an emotional scan regularly to deal with shit that is distracting you.

Take a moment and do an emotional scan. What seeds are you holding? Walkthrough the above process and either clean them out or destroy them. While you are holding on to those seeds, you are significantly reducing your happiness, your productivity, and your focus.

Nate had an argument with his co-worker, Jeff. This argument came after weeks of tense and terse interactions. The bottom line, Nate simply did not like Jeff. At all. He felt Jeff was a narcissistic bully that always put himself in the limelight, shoving others aside.

The argument came on a day when Nate couldn't handle it anymore. He had bit his tongue for weeks, allowing Jeff to "get away" with his actions until Nate couldn't hold it in any longer. The argument did not solve anything. On the contrary, it caused Nate to dislike Jeff even more. Tensions soared.

After reframing the situation, Nate requested a sit-down meeting with Jeff. During the meeting, Nate expressed his feelings without excusing Jeff. He simply owned his own feelings. He let Jeff know that in the future, in the presence of a negative situation, he was going to remove himself from the conversation versus engage in it.

Interestingly, when Nate chose not to engage, Jeff's episodes of being a jerk began to decrease.

Nate did not have to like Jeff, but he could not hold on to the negative emotions any longer. Confronting the issues and setting healthy and appropriate boundaries allowed Nate to put his focus on things that mattered.

Making Our Mind More Productive

We have looked at your environment and the impact of sensory and emotional distractions. Now let's go a step further and create the ideal *internal* environment for you to be productive.

To tap into our highest potential, we need to be able to shut off or minimize the distractions. The most efficient means of doing so is to meditate.

For some people, the mere thought of meditating invokes painful images of trying to sit still while not looking at their phone for an excruciating amount of time. It's just not realistic, they think. Are you kidding me? Sit still and do nothing? Do you know how long my to-do list is?

Before you get all metaphysical or defensive with me on this topic, let me challenge your thinking a bit.

Have you ever been in a situation where the outside world was shut out, even momentarily, and you had a great idea, solved a problem, remembered something that had been plaguing you, or the like? You were probably in a meditative state. And you were probably not even aware of it.

I struggle to relax and always have. There is some inner programming from my childhood that interferes with my ability just to sit down, rest, and do nothing. The thought of traditional *meditation* was not appealing to me. "I just can't quiet my mind," I would protest.

But then I started running a few years ago. On days that I didn't run, I would typically go out for a hike. I would jokingly refer to my runs or my hikes as my "therapy" because I genuinely felt so much better after, beyond just the nice dopamine hit.

When I ran, and when I hiked, my cell phone was off. I had no email dinging at me. Facebook wasn't taunting me. It was me, my feet, my music, and just time. The rhythmic sense of my footsteps. The comfort of being outside.

Let me tell you, I am a freaking creative, relaxed, and authentic genius when I am out there! I would create new products or services in my head, brainstorm concepts, resolve problems and issues, and work through discontent feelings. When I called it therapy, I was not joking. I felt the most open, vulnerable, and engaged than during any other part of my day.

"That's because you're meditating," a wise friend advised me. I struggled to agree with her.

It just didn't seem right to me. How can I be meditating when I'm exerting myself, sweating, and my heart is racing?

It is simple, she countered. The act of meditation is the act of blocking out and buffering yourself from external distractions, allowing yourself the ability to dig into your glorious subconscious. Consider when you are driving home, and next thing you know, you arrive. You don't remember driving on the freeway, taking your exit, or turning on your street. You were meditating. Your subconscious knew what to do.

I am not a natural runner nor a natural athlete. It takes work for me to run, and the most challenging aspect is my breathing. So as I run, I focus on each breath, the rhythm, the cadence. I match my breathing to the music, often singing along with my playlist to ensure I'm breathing well. My daughter taught me this trick from her days yelling cadence when she was in the Navy. And it works! I stopped thinking about trying to breathe and just focused on singing.

Just like every other human being on the face of the Earth, I cannot multitask. When my focus is on my breathing, I cannot possibly be talking on the phone, scrolling Facebook, or answering emails. I am just breathing. When I am singing, I am just singing and not focusing on my breathing.

And that's where the magic happens. As my breathing settles into a consistent cadence, my subconscious opens up. And it is incredible!! If I'm feeling creative, ideas start bubbling up. If I'm working through a problem, issue, or negative emotion, I begin to rationalize it, focusing on solutions or eliminating the negativity.

As soon as I would finish my run, I would capture notes on what I had just discovered and realized. I had a clear direction, clear thoughts, and clear emotions from which to manage the rest of my day.

With this experience, I then purposely planned my hikes as the ultimate team meeting with a team of three: me, myself, and I. With business development podcasts or leadership books loaded up on Audible, I would get lost in learning. My mind was completely open and receptive. And once again, all the distractions were gone. It was just me, the outdoors, the trail, and my footsteps. And maybe an occasional coyote or jackrabbit.

The obvious side benefit was that I was improving my strength and physical health at the same time I was working on my mental health. And that nice kick of endorphins and dopamine made Belinda a happy girl for quite a few hours after the hike concluded.

For those of you keeping score, yes, that's a win. A win. And a win.

Interestingly enough, once I recognized that I loved moving meditation, I began meditating the old-fashioned way: I sit quietly on my meditation pillow, burning some incense, listening to my little waterfall. And that is precious time invested in making me more balanced, open, and yes, productive.

Meditation can look different for everyone. Perhaps for you, it's a nice long bubble bath or a walk around the block (with your phone off). It could be a long drive or sitting on your porch watching the sunrise or sunset.

Meditation Activity

Identify a way that you can incorporate meditation into your daily life. Start with just 15 minutes. If you need to use a timer, use a timer.

During that time, eliminate all distractions. Focus just on your breath at first. Breathe in deeply, slowly exhale. Picture yourself breathing in peace, harmony, and clarity, and exhaling anything negative that you are holding on to.

If you can't sit that long, go for a walk – outside or on a treadmill. In a corporate environment, take the 15 minutes to go for a walk around the office building, or find a quiet spot to sit away from your desk.

When you begin to realize the incredible benefits of meditation, it can quickly become a habit, which is what I will be discussing in your next step!

Habit #4: Meditate daily in a way that works for you!

Making Our Body More Productive

I was at Chicago O'Hare airport recently, waiting at my gate to board my flight back to Phoenix. As I find people and their behavior fascinating, I frequently just look around and study them. As I scanned my fellow passengers at that moment, I realized that the vast majority had all assumed the same position.

You may be familiar with it: Hand raised, holding a phone. Eyes down, neck bent at an awkward angle. Just by observing the consistent postures, it was not hard to see that we are creating an inferior alignment structure that will lead to other issues. In the 15 minutes that I stood at the gate watching my fellow travelers, all but one individual maintained the neck-bent position for the entire time.

Experts are calling the resulting injury "text neck" – the neck pain and damage sustained from looking down at our cell phone, tablet, or other devices too frequently and for too long.

Symptoms associated with text neck include upper back pain, spasms, shoulder pain and tightness, and possibly neurological symptoms that radiate down the arm and into the hand.

To counteract text neck and other issues:

- Limit the time that you're looking down
- Move the device to be at eye-level
- Stretch! Throughout the day do neck, back and shoulder stretches

In today's modern work environments, it is not just our cell phones that are causing issues. It's our derrieres! We are sitting for hours upon hours. Let's go back in time to the way were designed. It was not with the intention of sitting for most of our waking hours. It was to run, hunt, gather, migrate, etc.

Sitting for extended periods invites a whole slew of problems. According to Edward Laskowski, M.D. of the Mayo Clinic, research has linked sitting for extended periods with health concerns such as obesity, increased blood pressure, high blood sugar and cholesterol levels, and excess fat around the waist. There is also an increased risk of death from cardiovascular disease and cancer.

In studies conducted, people that sat for extended periods but offset it with 60 to 75 minutes of moderately intense physical activity, countered the effects of the sitting.

Dr. Laskowski recommends the following:

- Every 30 minutes, stand-up and take a break
- Consider what activities you could do while standing up (such as taking a phone call)
- Instead of sitting in a conference room for a meeting, take a walk! (Win. Win. Win!)
- Use a standing or walking desk

Other problems can arise, such as circulation issues leading to varicose veins, getting DVTs (blood clots in your legs), and poor posture that can result in increased fatigue.

In the next step, I am going to guide you through some additional techniques to further your awareness of the body and productivity connection.

Key Take-Aways from Step Two:

1. Create an environment that minimizes sensory distractions. Turn off notifications and chimes. Reduce the number of windows you have open on your browser.

2. Do an inventory of your sensory sensitivities to stimulate productivity: visual, auditory, kinesthetic, olfactory, and gustatory.

3. Conduct a personal scan of your emotional distractions. Walkthrough the process to either destroy them or resolve them.

4. Practice meditation, in whichever form works best for you.

5. Be aware of your posture, including with your cell phone or other devices, and the amount of time that you spend sitting.

Belinda Goodrich

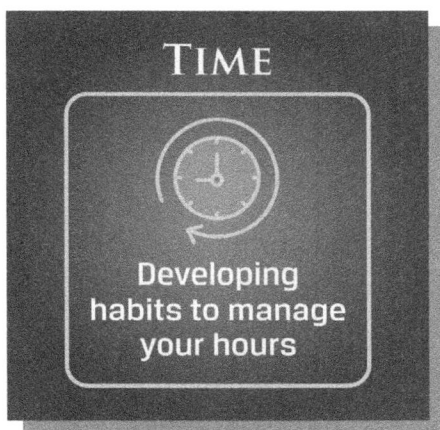

TIME

Developing habits to manage your hours

STEP 3: TIME

DEVELOPING THE MOST IMPORTANT HABITS TO MANAGE OUR HOURS

You have clarified your mission and goals and also evaluated the distractions that are preventing you from being as productive and fulfilled as you would like. In your third step, you will learn how to maximize the hours in the day through the intelligent application of your effort.

As you know, I cannot possibly give you more than 24 hours in a day. However, I can help you change your perspectives and, most importantly, your habits, to make the most of those 24 hours.

You take multiple actions throughout the day without being consciously aware of them. It just happens without a struggle or internal debate. These are our habits that are so subconsciously understood that there is no need for conscious involvement in the decision.

I started making my bed every day. Every. Single. Day. Even when I am on the road and staying in a hotel room. It signals the start of the day in an organized, predictable, and comforting way, and it gives me something to look forward to that night. You have to agree that there is nothing better than climbing into a nicely made bed at night.

But a made bed was not always nirvana to me. In fact, it was my nemesis because I struggled with severe insomnia. The bed represented stress and a struggle. However, one significant change in my life completely changed my relationship with my bed.

Manage Your Time by Managing Your Sleep

As I mentioned earlier in this book, I started running a few years ago. To be clear, I have never been a runner. Running was a challenge due to a nice case of being quite pigeon-toed. To further complicate the situation, I had the lungs of an 80-year old chain smoker. I did not have an ounce of athletic ability.

But I was determined to run for a couple of reasons. The first was that I had gone through a relatively traumatic health crisis, and I knew I had to turn things around. The second reason was a deep, emotional drive to run in honor of a young mother who had been killed by a drunk driver while out for a training run for the Boston Marathon.

Little-by-little, step-by-step, my miles started to increase. I got stronger and more confident. I started running 5ks, progressed to 10ks, and then tackled my first half marathon. A year later, I was training for my first full marathon at the age of 47.

The marathon was in November, which meant that the majority of my training miles would be happening during the summer. The challenge was that I lived in Phoenix, Arizona, where daytime high temperatures could soar well above 110 degrees. The only chance to get a run in without completely killing myself would be to get out there before the sun rose. Four days per week, including Sunday, I would set my alarm for 3:45 a.m. and be out the door by 4 a.m.

Let me tell you, I would sleep so good on those nights! This was especially exciting for me because I had struggled with insomnia for years. It was a horrible cycle of constant exhaustion, frustration, and even health issues. It got to the point that I started taking prescription sleeping pills to fall asleep and quickly became dependent on them.

With a strong family history of addiction, I knew I had to quit and quit cold turkey at that. And I did. It was brutal, and I was so envious of people who could just go to bed and go to sleep.

But that had now changed. I was sleeping great. I was waking up feeling alert, refreshed, and ready to take on the day. I was ecstatic that I was sleeping so well on the nights I ran, that I decided to set my alarm for 3:45 a.m. every single day of the week.

And eventually, it became a habit. My body got accustomed to waking up at the same time every day, which lead to me falling asleep close to the same time every night. I realized that the consistency of my sleep cycle tremendously improved my productivity, my health, and my entire mental state.

The detrimental effects of sleep deprivation have been scientifically studied for years. And yet, typical behavior actually put us into this no-win cycle of starting the week with a sleep deficit.

Callie was one of those girls that made others green with envy. She just appeared to have a never-ending supply of energy: from the moment she got up in the morning until the moment she went to bed, which was often late at night. She loved the fact that she needed very little sleep.

But as she got older, her body started to shift. Her behavior did not, however. She always looked forward to the weekends. With an extensive network of amazing friends, they would hit the town Friday and Saturday nights, closing down the bars. In response, she would sleep in until close to noon on both Saturday and Sunday.

Sunday evening, she tried to go to bed early, knowing she had a 6 a.m. alarm for work, but she just wasn't tired...yet.

When the alarm jumped her out of a sound sleep, she felt miserable. "Ugh, I hate Mondays," she'd say. As the pattern continued, she found herself getting sick more frequently, and she started gaining weight. She always felt as though she was playing catch-up with her sleep, never quite getting enough.

It was a hiking club that she joined that snapped her out of this sleep deprivation habit. Meeting at 7 a.m. on Saturdays and Sundays, she figured out pretty quickly that the hiking served her far better than the nights at the club. The consistency of her sleep-wake cycle gave her more energy, more focus, and she was back to her goal weight.

I believe that one of the most damaging things that we do to our bodies and our minds is not having the same sleep-wake cycle each day. I am not telling you to give up your social activities, because we need those too. But I am suggesting you keep a reasonably consistent wake-up time, even on the weekends.

By staying up late on Friday or Saturday, or whatever your nights off are, you are most likely starting your work with sleep deprivation. Of all days, when you need to be most on-point, you are exhausted to begin your workweek.

Not only is this causing issues with your engagement, innovation, and creativity, it is creating a negative experience, that your brain is now associating with "work." If every Monday you feel like crap, your mind believes that Mondays are bad because that is the day where you always feel like crap. This creates subconscious programming leading you to hate Mondays. No wonder you struggle with your mojo and motivation on Mondays!

I challenge you that Mondays should be awesome! A fresh start to a new week. They should not be dreaded but embraced. Forget what happened last week. It is a brand-new week to do some freaking awesome shit. Get out there and get after it! My favorite meme on the internet sums it up:

Do sharks complain about Monday?

No. They're up early.

Biting stuff. Chasing shit.

Being scary – reminding everyone they're a f$@%ing shark.

Be a shark, my friend. Say it out loud right now — screw who can hear you.

"I am a freaking shark! I don't complain about Monday; I attack it!"

Ok, now that you're a freaking shark, here is the habit you need to commit to doing:

Habit #5: Set your alarm for the same time seven days per week. And don't dawdle in bed. Jump out of that bed, like a shark on a mission. Get up and do something. Have a cup of coffee. Write in your journal. Watch the sunrise. Do something.

Impacts of Sleep Deprivation

Setting this habit is not just so that you like Mondays. Sleep deprivation is one of the most damaging and preventable impacts on our productivity. The prefrontal cortex is particularly susceptible to lack of sleep. And remember that is our thinking and logical brain that we desperately need to utilize.

How much sleep you need varies from person to person, but it typically ranges between 7 and 8 ½ hours per night. I am a bit of an oddball with sleep. When I was younger, I averaged 5 ½ hours per night to feel fully rested; now, I need about 6 ½ hours. While that seems low, I have learned to be very in-tune with my body and my sleep needs. When I need more than my usual sleep, I take it. I do not allow myself to function in a sleep-deprived state, as I literally cannot afford to – physically or mentally.

Two processes regulate our sleep: the homeostatic process S and our circadian process C. The homeostatic process is pretty straight forward – the longer we are awake, the more our need for sleep will increase.

There are two considerations with sleep deprivation; not only is it the impact on our cognitive function during the day, but also what our body is missing out on when we are not sleeping. You may think, "oh, I'm just tired," but it is so much more than that. While we are sleeping, our body goes through beautiful restitution, including tissue recovery, that we desperately need.

The impact of sleep deprivation during the day is much more palpable. Externally you will be more easily agitated, discouraged, and struggle with focus, memory, and cognitive function. Internally, the lack of sleep triggers the sympathetic nervous system. The result is a rise in your blood pressure and an increase in your cortisol secretion – your stress hormone. Your immunity responses can be weakened along with developing a resistance to insulin.

Back to my opening statement: people desire more hours in the day, something that is 100% impossible. Now, I am telling you that I want you to take some of those precious hours that you do have and devote it to more sleep. No, I am not kidding. As a matter of fact, I am dead serious.

Our productivity and mental health are suffering because we are not getting enough sleep. Plain and simple. The extra hour you devote to sleeping can more than double your effectiveness and productivity during the day. It is rather like making an investment that you can be guaranteed will make an immediate hefty return. While you may have fewer hours during which to get shit done, those hours are going to be so much more productive that you will actually have time left over!

Manage Your Time by Exploiting Your Circadian Rhythm

All living creatures have a natural circadian rhythm. It is called a rhythm because it is consistent. Day after day. Week after week.

When you understand your rhythm, you can structure your day in a way to maximize your productivity versus trying to fight against how your body is biologically wired.

Here's how it goes: Peak – Dip – Peak – Dip – Peak – Dip

The first peak in your performance and mental alertness occurs mid-morning. This is a time when you will have the highest mental acuity and is the best time for highly intellectual tasks. This is the ideal time for strategic decisions, highly technical pursuits, and topics that require focused attention. Typically, we have yet to be weighed down with the obstacles and challenges of the day, so we're not dealing with the same number of distractions that we will be later in the day. The peak begins to dip around lunchtime, bottoming out in the early afternoon.

Everyone is familiar with this dip, and oftentimes, we blame it on lunch. While some types of food can undoubtedly contribute to the dip, it is our essential biological wiring that gives the brain the message that it needs to rest and recover for a bit. This phenomenon has been around since human beings, in fact, all creatures existed. Thus, the love of the afternoon siesta! Our brain needs to rest.

Unfortunately, most employers aren't on the "hey, let's all take a nap!" bandwagon. You still have to work. So in response, this is the time and place to do something active. If you are going to have a meeting, make it a walking or active meeting, even if it's just around your office. Or stand and make your phone calls. If you are lucky enough to have a gym on-site, take a 30-minute stroll on the treadmill while catching up on some pertinent reading. Move or rest. Those are the options during this dip.

Mid-afternoon, we experience another peak. But this one looks different than the morning peak because our brains are in a different state. While we can still think analytically, we are also much more creative. Our defenses are down a bit, and we allow more ideas and free-thinking. This is the perfect time for more creative pursuits and brainstorming.

I learned this in a fascinating manner. I have written several very technical books, and my prime writing time is first thing in the morning. When I started to work on my memoir, I stuck to my practiced writing routine of writing in the morning. But it was just not working for me. I could recite facts of my life, but I had a challenging time ascribing emotion and experiences to the events. Some negative self-talk began. You know the drill on this, right? "I suck. I'm no good. I'm stupid."

Then one day, I happened to have a nice 3-hour chunk of time available in the afternoon, and I decided to try again with the memoir. It just began flowing. Thinking it was a fluke, I tried it again the next day. Rinse and repeat. Bingo! I realized just how impactful my personal circadian rhythm was and have since done my best to align with it — technical stuff in the morning, creative things in the afternoon.

After our little creativity peak in the afternoon, we experience another dip. Luckily, this typically coincides with our drive home, fetching the kids, making dinner, and all of those fun household obligations. (And I am saying *fun* seriously, not sarcastically. They should be fun. There is nothing more important than family and home. This is where you should be refilling your "joy" tank!)

Now, here is something interesting. We get another peak in the evening. For many people, our phone is quieter, our emails slow down, and we are not dealing with the daily distractions of our offices. I recommend creating a routine during this time: journal about your day, plan the following day, and do your gratitude acknowledgments and affirmations.

And then finally, our last dip is where our body is saying, "ok, buddy, you're done. Time to get some rest." Listen to it and go to bed. Get that sleep that your body so desperately needs!

This is a rhythm, which means that it happens the same way seven days per week, 52 weeks out of the year. When we alter our sleep-wake pattern, such as sleeping in on the weekend, we are fighting against our natural biological wiring.

For 90% of people, this is the general cycle, and then there is the other 10%, me included, that has an earlier or later orientation. I am what is known as a "lark," a very early morning person. My peaks and dips shift earlier, with my prominent intellectual peak occurring around 7:00 am versus 9:00 or 10:00 a.m. "Owls" are those people whose circadian is shifted on the latter end of the day. Interestingly, my father was a lark, and my mother was most definitely an owl. Apparently, the lark gene ran strong!

Habit #6: Identify your natural circadian rhythm and then manage your day and your tasks to align with that rhythm.

The Magic of Water

You have heard it over and over again. Ad nauseum. Drink your damn water. I know you know. But I am going to give you some additional insight to make that great big bottle of water even more tempting.

When the water craze first started happening, I thought it was bizarre. I grew up in Maine. We had a well. And a hose. And a faucet. We would never consider *buying* water. It seemed like a hilarious prank: "Ha ha ha, someone put water in a bottle, and they are *selling* it! Who would buy that?"

But we do buy it! A 2019 Beverage Industry article states that 72% of Americans "say bottled water, still and/or sparkling, is among their most preferred non-alcohol beverage." And in the US, for the third year in a row, bottled water is the number one packaged beverage.

So yay us! We are buying water (still seems a little weird, even though I am now a self-professed water snob), and we are drinking water.

But we need to have a more in-depth discussion on it as relates to productivity, which is, after all, why you are reading this book. Water consumption has a significant impact on productivity because of its effect on our body and specifically, our brain.

As an adult, you are made up of about 60% water. The blood that is coursing through your body is a beautiful 90% water. On average, you will get about 20% of your daily water intake from food, but the rest you must drink!

The National Academies of Sciences, Engineering, and Medicine recommends a daily intake of 125 ounces for men and 91 ounces for women.

There are three critical benefits to maintaining a healthy water intake. First of all, it aides us in getting rid of waste in our body. Yes, I'm talking about peeing and pooping. Get that crap out of you, pun intended. Secondly, being hydrated allows us to regulate our body temperature. Living in Arizona, this is why I compulsively drink water without even being conscious of it. Triple-digit degree days have a way of zapping your hydration.

But it is the last significant benefit that I want to discuss because most people are familiar with the first two benefits. Water is crucial in helping our brain function. Drinking water boosts our metabolism, which in turn boosts our energy levels. One study quoted by Healthline found that drinking two cups of water raised the metabolic rate by 30%, and that increase lasted over an hour. Think about that! It's like a nice shot in the arm with no adverse side effects!

Just a bit ago, I mentioned that you are 60% water, but did you know your brain is 75% water? With the optimal hydration level in your brain, you can think faster, be more focused, and have better clarity and creativity. So consider something: by the time your body feels thirsty, your brain is already dehydrated. Be proactive with your fluid intake.

Research published in the *American Journal of Clinical Nutrition* reinforces this. In evaluating the study participants, they found that as little as <1% drop in body mass from water loss impacted brain function – specifically memory and attention. Those without the recommended hydration also experienced feelings of anxiety and depression.

Here are a couple of considerations:

- Your intake of water should be consistent throughout the day, so you are not getting yourself to the point of dehydration, hydration, dehydration, on repeat. Keep yourself at the optimal level with a consistent intake throughout the day.

- Most likely, you go through the night (8+ hours) with minimal, if any, water intake. This means you are starting the day at a deficit. Now, if you are like me, you may roll out of bed and stumble to the coffee maker. While the caffeine is a diuretic, drinking coffee still gives you a net hydrating effect (that's the good news!) But you should always take in a nice big glass of water upon waking to get you in balance even quicker.

- Diet beverages do not equal hydration. As a recovered Diet-Cokaholic, I can preach on this one. Suffice to say, my kidneys, brain, and skin celebrated when I started replacing my daily habit of two liters of Diet Coke with water. Thankfully we now have a lot of healthier options, such as flavored sparkling water (just watch the sodium).

- If you travel a lot, increase your intake even if you are like my best friend and hate peeing on an airplane. Deal with it and drink water!

- If you drink alcohol, increase your intake. If you are overtired, increase your intake. If you are working out, increase your intake. If you have to put some serious brainpower into a task, increase your intake.

Habit #7: Drink the recommended ounces of water per day, adjusting for situations that may require you to increase your intake. Start the day with a nice, refreshing glass of water!

Straighten Up and Fly Right

This was one of my mother's favorite sayings. It was typically directed at us when we were not behaving appropriately. "You better straighten up and fly right, girl. Or else." I am going to say the same thing to you, but in the literal sense. Let's talk about our posture. I am super sensitive to this because of an unfortunate event early in life.

I remember being in junior high and being incredibly shy, awkward, and self-conscious, as are most girls at that age. And boys, for that matter! I had been trying to make friends with the cool girl in school. She oozed self-confidence, and everyone thought she was terrific. If you have seen the movie Mean Girls, she was the Regina George of Bonny Eagle High School. And I so desperately wanted to be her friend.

We had just changed for gym class and were noisily making our way to the gymnasium. The gym teacher instructed us to line up, and I was excited to be next to the cool girl, Jennifer. This was my chance to become her friend. She looked at me and smiled. And then said, "You walk like you have a stick stuck up your butt."

Smack. Devastation. Embarrassment. I was already pigeon-toed, which many of the kids pointed out, and now I find out I look like I have a stick up my butt. Seriously?

It's been 38 years, and I can remember that exact moment like it was yesterday. It was so heavy with emotion that it got programmed deep, deep in my subconscious. In reaction, I was hyper-focused on tucking my tailbone in and under, almost creating a hunchback appearance. Even as an adult, I will periodically flashback to that moment and think, "Oh no, do I have a stick up my butt?" and quickly alter my posture.

I now speak on stage in front of hundreds of people and wouldn't you know it, that thought still comes up. And I'll feel myself adjust. It's crazy the impact of 11 words, 38 years ago.

But then a dear friend of mine was presenting on the importance of posture when you are a speaker. She had us stand up and, with a few simple instructions, had us standing taller, stronger, and prouder. Her years as a classically trained ballet dancer taught her the criticality of proper posture.

A 2017 study in the *Journal of Behavior Therapy and Experimental Psychology* concluded that "adopting an upright posture may increase positive affect, reduce fatigue and decrease self-focus" in people with mild to moderate depression. Proper posture leads to higher self-esteem, a higher level of alertness, and a better mood.

Essentially, when you stand up straight, tall, and proud, you are sending a signal to your brain and your subconscious that you are strong, balanced, and capable!

There are apparent psychological benefits to having good posture, but there are also physiological benefits. When we stand up straight, we can breathe easier. Our breathing becomes more effective because the diaphragm has enough space in the thoracic cavity to fully expand and contract. And we need oxygen to restore and rejuvenate cells.

Habit #8: Every 25 minutes, do a posture check. Take in a nice deep breath and straighten up. Envision yourself, opening up with confidence, and sending vital oxygen to your body and brain. And notice how confident you feel!

The first three steps have set you up to physically and emotionally engage in your life and your productivity. You have a clear mission and goals, you have set-up your ideal environment, and you have learned techniques to allow you to be more productive within the hours that you have for the day. Notice that I have not told you to buy a planner, write a to-do list, or anything of that sort? This book is about making fundamental changes to your body, brain, and habits. That is the only way that you will change your productivity.

But no worries, in the next section, you will move into activation. Steps four, five, and six are all focused on your day-to-day methods and techniques for creating consistent and healthy patterns and results.

Key Take-Aways from Step Three:

1. Prioritize creating healthy sleep habits. Do not start the week in a deficit by altering your wake-sleep patterns on the weekend. Stick to a consistent wake-up time whenever possible.

2. Allow your circadian rhythm to dictate your energy

allocation during the day, scheduling activities based on your peaks and dips.

3. Hydrate, hydrate, hydrate. Do so consistently throughout the day, making allowances for changing circumstances, such as sleeping, traveling, workouts, hea⁻, etc.

4. Understand the power and connection with your posture, both psychologically and physiologically. Don't worry – you won't look like you have a stick up your butt. I promise!

Section 2

Activate

Steps 4 - 6

Belinda Goodrich

STEP 4: INSULATE

CREATING YOUR PRODUCTIVITY COCOON

Now here's where the book gets tough. You are aware of where you want to go, who you want to be, and set yourself up for success. But now you have to do all of those things, consistently, to make the changes you desire in your life. And this is what separates the professionals from the amateurs.

The first thing you need to do is ask yourself, do you want to change?

I recently surveyed over 500 people from various occupations. The majority of the respondents claimed that their lives had improved somewhat or significantly over the last three years. I was somewhat surprised by this as most people I talk with are frustrated, tired, and burnt out.

However, that same group reported the following:

- 83% had issues with weight gain, obesity, high blood pressure, diabetes, or increases in cholesterol
- 71% struggled with depression and/or anxiety
- 69% had to seek medical attention for symptoms related to stress

That indicates that we believe that our lives our improving with this always-on society, yet our bodies are screaming an entirely different message.

So again, ask yourself, do you want to make a change? What is the driver of that change?

In the words of my beloved Uncle Reggie, you, my friend, are "too precious to waste." I want you living a joyful life, not stressed out and burnt out.

Protecting Your Productivity

In Step Two, you took steps to create an environment of productivity. But as the world, and our lives go, preserving that productivity is going to be challenging. But it is also doable.

In Step Four, we are going to work on your inner resolve and outward actions that will be needed to insulate yourself from those distractions for you to focus.

Physical Insulation

We receive feedback from the world five ways: sight, smell, taste, touch, and listening. When it comes to physical insulation, all of these senses need to be considered.

Remember that your body and brain are continuously scanning the environment to see if there is something that deserves attention. Think about your workspace and list out the top distractions you experience during the day, considering all of your senses.

(For example, the temperature of the room, the sounds of your co-workers, a messy desk or workspace, etc.)

DISTRACTION	SENSE	INTENSITY

I would recommend increasing your awareness for a few days to inventory what distractions are occurring and how severe they are.

Now go back through your list and identify your top three most impactful distractions. Identify some strategies for eliminating or minimizing them below:

_____

_____

_____

_____

_____

_____

_____

We all know that our cell phone is one of our challenging distractions. We all have them, and many of us are entirely dependent upon them. Have you thought you lost your phone and had that moment of sheer panic?

Here is something to consider, 25 years ago we did not have a phone attached to us all the time. We still functioned. The world continued to spin. It was glorious!

And we keep finding ways to increase our "always-on," such as smartwatches! There is something comical about the fact that I now get a message on my watch on my left wrist from the cell phone I'm holding in my right hand. The watch vibrates, the phone chimes, almost simultaneously. No, we don't have a problem.

I spend a fair amount of time in the air, flying to various locations around the world. While most people hate flying, I love it. Well, to be honest, I actually have a fear of flying, BUT I love flying because it is my crucial productivity time! I get so much shit done on planes and in the airline lounge.

Think about it: on the plane, my cell phone is off, and I typically do not buy Wi-Fi, so no email, no social media temptation. On top of it, I am an utterly anti-social flyer. It is my time to be entirely in my zone. I get on the plane and immediately put in my headphones, queue up my playlist, and put up an invisible barrier between me and any seatmates. It is fantastic.

Add to the equation the fact that I typically fly out on early flights; I am also hitting my peak productivity window from a circadian perspective.

So ideally, you are creating that same type of bubble-wrap effect around you when you are focusing on valuable work.

Tina had been employed by the local utility company for 15 years. She loved her job and loved her co-workers. She was considered the "mama" of the office not only because of her attitude of support but because she kept everyone in line. She knew pretty much everything about everything in the building. If you needed something, you went to Tina.

As the company grew and technology advanced, Tina began feeling more and more overwhelmed. She would struggle juggling everything that she had to do, let alone help everyone else out that stopped by her desk. Which, by the way, was conveniently / inconveniently situated between the main entrance and the break room. She was in the most heavily traveled corridor for the office.

Tina found herself getting more short-tempered, and her immunity began to weaken. After yet another nasty illness, Tina knew things had to change.

After a blunt discussion with her manager, Tina moved to a cubicle in a quieter location. She also blocked out her calendar with her work times, offering small windows of time that she would be available to help others. She laughingly called these her "office hours" and would put out a "The Doctor Is In!" sign on the outside of her cube when she was open for helping others. During her work blocks, she would close out her email and her instant messaging program.

At first, Tina allowed herself to feel bad about having boundaries, but as her work and health improved, she recognized just how valuable it was.

Tips for reducing physical distractions:

- Schedule blocks of time where you will have your email open and sending notifications, perhaps three times per day.

- Turn off phone notifications for social media and other applications during defined work periods.

- Whether you work in an office, work at home, are an entrepreneur or a stay-at-home parent, set defined and consistent office hours. Schedule your different responsibilities using a calendaring system.

- Identify your ideal background noise. For some people it's music. Maybe it is white noise from a fan or air purifier.

Or perhaps it's the hustle and bustle of a public location. Identify your ideal and complementary environmental sounds that allow you to focus.

- Experiment with essential oils either in a diffuser or on your wrist. Now that I have used the "Focus" blend consistently, just the smell of it gives my brain the message that it is time to work.

Emotional Insulation

As I mentioned in Step 2, physical distractions are a lot easier to deal with than emotional disturbances. You can shut off your phone, but you cannot as easily just shut off your emotions.

First and foremost, regularly conduct an emotional scan. Where are your thoughts? Do you have a lingering issue or negative state associated with a person? If so, it needs to be confronted and addressed. Can it be resolved or not? If not, make a conscious effort to let it go, giving yourself grace and peace.

If it can potentially be resolved, talk to the person, or take whatever steps are necessary to move towards resolution. It is surprising to me how often just an open line of communication can change the situation completely.

You know how you just *know* when someone does not like you? I had that situation recently with a professional peer. There was no mistaking the vibe she gave off. She did not like me. Maybe it was the dirty looks, the condescending remarks, or the way she went out of her way to avoid me that gave me that message. It was evident not only to me but everyone who interacted with the two of us.

I let my dismay and discomfort fester to the point that I manifested how much I disliked her. I disliked someone because they disliked me. Sounds a bit childish, doesn't it? It drove me crazy that I did not know why she was upset with me. It thoroughly pervaded my mental state when we were in the same room or at the same event.

I like to say that I am a very classic Libra. I do not want anything being out of balance. And I really do not like anyone being upset at me. Finally, I could not take it anymore and decided to be a mature adult and confront her.

We scheduled a Zoom call, and I was grateful she accepted. Immediately upon connecting, she proceeded to tell me that she knew I was anti-Semite. I was utterly astounded. I can be called a lot of things, accused of doing a lot of things, but one thing I am not is prejudice to any race or religion or any other personal belief system. I was incredibly blessed to be raised by a mother who openly discussed different beliefs with us and taught us to understand, be curious, and love and support others.

I could not even be angry. I was way too hurt. It was the most personal and unfounded attack I had faced. She based this assessment on the fact that when she let me know she was Jewish, I started treating her poorly. Specifically, I chaired a committee that opted to have our holiday party at a different home than hers.

Looking back, I don't even know quite how I managed to respond to her accusations, but I'm sure I sputtered on about how ludicrous it was. I found myself creating a defense by telling her about all of my friends that are not of my faith: atheists, Hindus, Muslims,

Jews, Catholics. I have always loved exploring other beliefs.

By the end of the call, I was calmer, and she seemed a bit more receptive, although I could sense some lingering doubt. But after our discussion, while hurt and offended, I was able to move beyond the stress of the relationship. I recognized there was absolutely nothing I could do to change her perception of me. I cannot control another's state of being, understandings, or beliefs. It was out of my control. I felt comfortable that I had done all that I could to resolve the situation.

If you find yourself in a similar situation, do not let it fester as long as I did. If your gut or your intuition is telling you that something is going on, you are most likely not just being paranoid. Something is going on, and it may be just a simple misunderstanding. Talk to the involved parties.

And then you may decide, like in my situation, that there is nothing more you can do. Give yourself permission to move on and move past it. Dig the seed out. It does not serve you.

Many people like to develop supportive affiliate networks. Again, this is a core survival mechanism. We want to be around people who think like us, act like us, and look like us because deep in our unconscious caveman brain, we believe that offers us protection. *However*, resist the urge to create your band of believers, your tribe of affiliates that will continue to hash and re-hash the negative situation with you. Every time you bring it back up, you put your emotional state right back into that negative space. Let that shit go.

Emotional Inventory Assessment

Notice during what situations, on what days, and during what hours you have different emotional states.

In the movie Office Space, one of the overly joyful characters is talking to her grumpy co-worker. "Oh, someone has a case of the Mondays!". As I mentioned previously, we are conditioned to dislike Mondays, or whatever the first day of your workweek may happen to be. Remember that is because we frequently associate the day with being overtired and overwhelmed.

When you identify those negative state-inducing patterns, take direct and immediate action to reframe it and release it. Guard your heart, my friend. Know your triggers and work diligently to change that mindset.

You can look at the sunrise and think, "damn, it's too early to be up!" or "wow, the beautiful promise of an entirely new day, and I'm lucky enough to be awake to see it."

You can look at Monday as a horrid ball and chain dragging behind you or as the ultimate day of reset, an opportunity to set the stage for an awesome week.

You can look at work as something to be dreaded or as a means of living the life of your choosing.

"Between stimulus and response, there is a space. And it is in that space that we have the power to choose our response. In our response lies our growth and our freedom." Viktor Frankl

When you have that next emotional distraction, remember that it is you who has the freedom to choose the response!

Just Say "No"

Ok, this is a tough one for a lot of people. Learn to say "NO." It is one of your most critical tools for crafting a life of fulfillment. While I do not want to generalize, we do typically find that this is more of an issue with women. Women have traditionally served in roles as caretakers. This is because biologically we are the gender that gives birth and nurtures the young – protecting the viability of the species.

Amy was a rockstar at work. Everyone adored her and her kind and gentle nature. She was smart, engaged, and warm. I first met Amy when I was called in to consult on their project and program management practices at her company. She was a love!

But behind her kind eyes, I saw a woman on the brink of a complete breakdown. She was utterly exhausted. As she began to review the project management procedures and systems with me, I interrupted her.

"How many hours do you work each week?" I questioned.

"Oh boy, I guess about 60-ish, I suppose," she responded with a quiet sigh.

"And when was the last time you had time off?" I continued.

"Well, I was supposed to go on a weekend getaway with my husband recently, but we have the big convention coming up, and I did not feel comfortable leaving." She looked at me apologetically.

I got the sense she was not apologizing for not taking her weekend away, but instead, she was apologizing for even considering going. "Why do you work so many hours?"

She looked at me with a mix of embarrassment and confusion. "Well, it's my job. There is work to be done." And with that, she started to crumble. She went on to explain that she had gained 40 pounds in the last six months, her blood pressure was high, and she was struggling with fatigue. At 31 years old, she felt like she was an old woman.

My heart broke for her, and I realized that if things did not change and change soon, the company was going to lose Amy, either to another company or to illness.

After more discussions, I learned that Amy felt she could not say 'no' to the requests that came her way. "Well, if I don't do them, who is going to?" she defended.

I coached Amy that as long as she did not refuse, they were going to continue to give her more work. It is a fundamental (and flawed) perspective of many businesses: if the work is getting done, why would they change anything? Her company was not going to reduce her workflow proactively. And they were most definitely not going to stop giving her more and more work.

The reality of the situation was dire, and I made it clear that it was her responsibility to take action. She absolutely could not continue the way she was going without serious detriment to her health and her relationships.

I did not take on her company as a client, recognizing that it was a no-win situation. Changing their processes and systems would not do anything to improve their project outcomes. This was a people issue, not a process issue. And it was pervasive throughout the company, from the CEO down to the lower levels.

About two months after my consultation with Amy's company, she sent me a message. She learned she was expecting a baby, and that was when she knew things had to change. She quit her job and started with a new organization. She practices saying no and has become adept at insulating herself. She is healthy, thriving, and proud of the work she is doing.

Saying no can be tough. You may feel guilty. You may "feel bad." But remember you control those feelings. If you are going to be the best *YOU* you can be, you have to protect, nurture, and care for yourself first. And the most significant step is saying "no"!

Remember, you have to put on your oxygen mask first to help others with theirs.

Habit #9: Commit to putting your oxygen mask on first before helping others. Repeat after me: "Just Say No!"

Reminders and Course Correction

To keep yourself as insulated as possible, always know where you are going and why you are going there. Having a clear picture of your destination protects you from your distractions and allows you to refocus quickly. This where a visual anchor such as a vision board or particular image can be so powerful. My vision board is strategically placed in my direct sightline, and I find myself glancing at it throughout the day – reminding myself of what I want in life.

When I am working on a new project or a new book, I place a visual of it on my phone and my computer. As I'm writing this very chapter, the wallpaper and lock screen on my phone and my laptop is a mockup of this very book. When I see it, I surge with pride, focus, and motivation to get it completed.

One of my happy places is on the water. I feel completely at peace, and it truly is therapeutic for my soul. I love getting my kayak in the water, exploring the shoreline, and just being in nature.

As I push off with my kayak, I'll have a section of the lake in mind to explore and start moving in that direction. Now, as I paddle, my path may shift to the right, so I paddle harder on the right side to course correct. In paddling harder on the right side, I may start going too much to the left, so I switch my focus and paddle harder on the left side.

And in this zig-zag fashion, I eventually make it to my desired destination.

When I find myself zigging or zagging, I don't get discouraged, tell myself I'm a failure and throw my paddle overboard. Of course, not! The zigs and the zags are simply feedback. They are messages to help me right my path.

That, my friend, is also how we need to navigate life. It will never be a straight line to our desired destination. Hell no! It will be a series of zigs and zags. Some zigs will be little; some will be huge. Some zags will be discouraging; some will be encouraging. But your zigs and your zags are absolutely, 100% NOT failures. They are feedback only.

Habit #10: When things don't go as planned, do not assess it as a failure. Reframe it as simply feedback.

Hopefully, you can see why Step One of GET IT DONE was defining your goals. When I'm kayaking, my goal is to reach a particular area of the lake. If I had no intention, I'd just be paddling aimlessly. And that is what so many of us do in this life. We just paddle aimlessly.

Key Take-Aways from Step Four:

1. Once you have identified and created your ideal environment for productivity, viciously protect it! My youngest daughter is a hockey goalie, and one of my proudest mom moments was when another parent commented that my girl was like a vicious bulldog on a short chain protecting her crease. Yes! Be a vicious bulldog!

2. Identify your most damaging distractions and put a plan in place to counteract, minimize, or eliminate those distractions.

3. Periodically conduct an emotional scan. What do you have brewing beneath the surface, and it is something that may be able to be resolved? If so, deal with it directly. If not, let it go.

4. Remember that you are always in control of your emotions. You cannot control the situation. You cannot control other people. But you can control your reaction and response.

5. Say "No" – loud and proud!

6. Embrace the zigs and the zags. They are feedback, not failures.

Belinda Goodrich

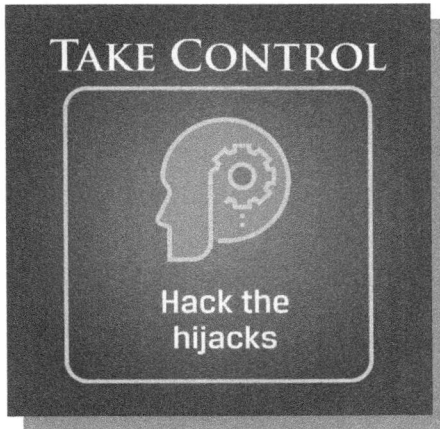

TAKE CONTROL

Hack the
hijacks

STEP 5: TAKE CONTROL

HACK THE HIJACKS

The intention of GET IT DONE is not just to cram more into your day. The intention is just the opposite. It is to create fluidity and flexibility within your day to apply your effort towards those actions that will create the ideal outcomes. This is the essence of intelligent productivity versus ignorant overwhelm.

You have been provided with techniques to isolate yourself as much as possible from physical and emotional distractions. The next step is to learn to work with your body and mind versus working against it.

In this step, you will leverage your understanding of the brain to create new neural pathways, hack an amygdala hijack, and understand your emotional intelligence. It is time to take control, fully involving and invoking the conscious and logical part of your brain.

The Gift of Neuroplasticity

When I moved to Phoenix from the northeast, I was pleasantly surprised by the layout of the streets. Phoenix was designed as a grid: streets on the east side of Central Avenue, avenues on the west side. Numbered roads run north and south whereas the named roads run east and west. Every main intersection is one mile. It is relatively impossible to get lost in Phoenix.

Compare that to the city of Boston. If you have ever attempted to drive in Boston, unless you are a Boston-native, you encountered some crazy roads, with no apparent rhyme or reason. While the locals like to joke that it is just to mess with out-of-towners, especially those from New York City, the truth is much more interesting. At least I think so.

Before Boston was a city, it was farmland and pastures for cows. Cows are just like any other species and are going to travel the path of least resistance. So, as they moved around, seeking out some fresh grazing, they would take the easiest route to the new pastures. As they walked, they started to create paths. The more they walked, the more defined those paths became, and the easier it was travel.

It is those cow paths that formed the first roads of Boston. So indeed, you are driving on the paths of least resistance, although it may be a struggle to see them as such in today's world!

The concept of how the Boston roads were formed, though, is the same concept as neuroplasticity. Neural pathways are well-trodden paths that actually do bear fruit. And the more we use them, the easier they are to use. This is how we can create new habits, like making the bed or working out every morning. All it takes is the will to commit to something, do it regularly, and it becomes a new path. This includes changing behaviors and changing thoughts.

If you want to create a new habit, you absolutely must stop thinking about the old habit. Your focus needs to shift entirely to the new habit. When I get out of bed in the morning, I think about my workout, not about lying in bed longer. I have shifted my focus to the benefits of the exercise versus the comfort of staying in bed. Your thoughts become your actions.

In 1949, Donald Hebb discovered that when "neurons fire together," they wire together. So if you are thinking about stress and feeling stressed, your stress pathways get strengthened. You can see how powerful this is when we replace negative thoughts and feelings with positive thoughts and feelings. Not only are we able to create new neural pathways, but the old, unused ones also begin to disintegrate without use!

Strengthening the new neural pathways takes consistency and repetition. At first, these paths are fragile. If a cow walks over the hill the same way two days in a row, a path begins to be created. But if she decides to opt-out of the hill for a few days or a week, that path begins to disappear. So, it is within our brains. Scientists estimate it can take anywhere from three to six months for those paths to be sufficiently strengthened.

Destructive Habit Exercise:

Identify five destructive habits or behavior patterns that inhibit your productivity and fulfillment:

Example   *I spend too much time on Facebook*

Habit 1   _____

Habit 2   _____

Habit 3   _____

Habit 4   _____

Habit 5   _____

For each of the identified habits, write down how it negatively impacts your life. Be explicit and detailed in describing those impacts.

Example   Being on Facebook wastes time that I should be applying to other tasks. I am embarrassed that I am on there as much as I am. I feel bad about myself when I compare my life to my friends that are doing better than me.

Habit 1 _____

_____

Habit 2 _____

_____

Habit 3 _____

_____

Habit 4 _____

_____

Habit 5 _____

_____

Now re-write these habits with the opposite state that you are striving to achieve:

Example ___*I prioritize my time, choosing to stay focused on tasks that get me closer to my goals.*___

Habit 1 _____

Habit 2 _____

Habit 3 _____

Habit 4 _____

Habit 5 _____

Get It Done!

Visualize and write down the positive impacts of your new habits.
Be explicit and detailed in describing those impacts:

Example: *I am fully engaged in making choices about where I spend my time. I am excited to see my progress against my goals. I feel confident, focused, and productive.*

Habit 1 _____

_____

Habit 2 _____

_____

Habit 3 _____

_____

Habit 4 _____

_____

Habit 5 _____

_____

I want you to pick the most damaging and powerful habit now and follow these instructions explicitly. Make this your priority and focus over the coming days:

1. Write the negative habit on the front of a piece of paper.

2. On the backside of it, write the negative impacts.

3. On a new piece of paper, write the new positive replacement habit.

4. On the back, write the positive benefits that you are going to achieve.

5. DESTROY that first sticky note. Burn it, rip it up, flush it down the toilet. You are no longer focusing on that habit. You are going to be applying 100% of your energy to the replacement habit.

6. Once you have started to wear a good neural pathway on that, repeat the steps for the next damaging habit.

7. You've got this! Each moment, each hour, each day, it will absolutely get easier.

Hack the Hijack

A key component of re-training the brain is understanding how to make the hormones and neurotransmitters work for us versus work against us. There are four that I specifically recommend tackling: dopamine, serotonin, oxytocin, and endorphins.

Now, of course, please do not take this section as medical advice. I am *not* a doctor, nor have I played a doctor on T.V. In some circumstances, people need to seek professional advice for issues with these neurotransmitters and hormones! This is not intended to replace professional help.

Dopamine

Dopamine is a neurotransmitter that enables us to feel pleasure. I call it the great motivator! It helps us strive for challenges, focus on tasks, and seek out interesting things. It is dopamine that pushes us to that finish line and puts that medal around our neck when we cross it. New research has revealed that dopamine not only engages us to seek pleasure, it also motivates us to avoid pain.

When our dopamine increases, we have increased pleasure. That pleasure than motivates us to repeat the same action to feel the pleasure again. This is the pleasure cycle that is experienced as exacerbated by addicts. Their need to continue to experience that pleasure drives the addiction: the more they have, the more they want. This is one of the reasons it is difficult to overcome an addiction.

When our levels of dopamine are low, we experience self-doubt, we procrastinate, and we may lack enthusiasm. If our lives are devoid of fulfillment and pleasure, our dopamine levels are low. And a negative feedback cycle ensues: I have no motivation, so I procrastinate. Then I feel bad that I am not getting more done. And on the cycle goes.

Here are some easy hacks to increase your dopamine:

1. Celebrate the small wins with incremental goals and microbites of work. There is nothing more gratifying than crumpling up a sticky note with a completed task and throwing that sucker in the trash! We will talk more about microbites in the next step.

2. Keep a file of your "wins." Write down your accomplishments, big and small. Keep a journal next to your bed, and each night write down what you accomplished that day.

3. Define what is next, giving yourself something always to get excited about.

4. Eat healthily: increase your protein intake and decrease your saturated fat.

5. Practice healthy habits such as exercising regularly, meditating, and getting enough sleep.

Serotonin

Serotonin is our happy chemical. When our serotonin is high, we feel happy, significant, and important. This is our uplifter, our cheerleader.

Used to transmit messages between nerve cells, serotonin serves many functions, but it has a crucial role in maintaining our mood balance.

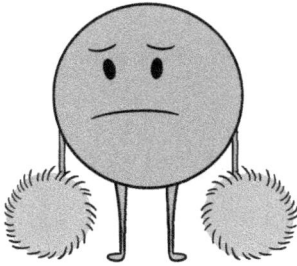

Low levels of serotonin have been related to depressive disorders, although it is not known if the low serotonin causes depression or if the depressive state causes low levels of serotonin. Decreased levels also have been found to cause fatigue.

Here is the crazy thing about serotonin; our limbic system does not distinguish between present time reality and a memory. Meaning that if you conjure up a memory of a time where you did something really well or felt accomplished, you will receive a nice little bolus of serotonin. This is one of the many reasons why gratitude journaling is so effective.

Try some of these hacks to increase your serotonin:

1. Altering your mood to create a positive emotional state. I hate to run, but I learned to smile while I was running. It tricked my brain into believing I was enjoying the activity. As a result, I started to actually enjoy it (thanks to the increase in serotonin!).

2. Get outside and get some sunshine! People that suffer from seasonal affective disorder (SAD) struggle with low serotonin levels due to the lack of sunlight during the cold or rainy seasons.

3. Meditate and re-live a happy and positive moment. During your meditation, invoke all of the senses that were involved in the original situation.

4. Eat foods that are high in tryptophans (tryptophan is a necessary ingredient in the production of serotonin): such as turkey, cheese, eggs, and salmon.

5. Consistently write in a gratitude journal. And smile when you write down all of those things in your life that you are grateful for having!

Oxytocin

This hormone is the lover! Our little buddy, oxytocin, enables us to build trust and intimacy with people and allows us to strengthen our relationships. This is our

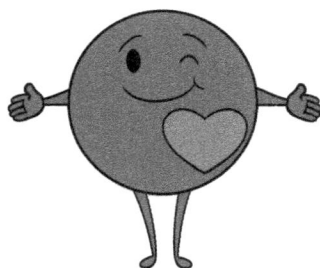

connector, connecting you with others around you.

It is oxytocin that plays a critical role in mothers bonding with their newborn infants. But it is not only found in women. For both genders, oxytocin plays a role in intimacy and sexual bonding in our adult relationships. We can also credit oxytocin with improving our social skills, our generosity, and our protective instincts.

When we have low levels of oxytocin, we feel isolated and rejected. Consider gym class in elementary school. I always dreaded when the class was divided into teams. Each team would have one captain, and they would alternate picking their team members from those kids that remained on the line.

Let's just say I was never picked in the first few rounds. It definitely induces the feeling of rejection! I was getting no oxytocin from my friends!

Here are some great hacks for increasing your oxytocin:

1. Oxytocin is about bonding and connecting, and that can happen as simple as giving someone a handshake. The physical contact of your hands creates a release of oxytocin.

2. If you want to really up your oxytocin game, then hug someone. Some experts even go so far as to recommend a minimal hugging goal for the day. Now, I would be remiss not to address the obvious with this one. Please do not hug someone that is not equally into the hugging, especially in light of our current environment and tensions around sexual advances and inappropriate touching. And yes, it is sad I have even to issue that warning. So hug your family, hug your friends, hug your loved ones, but not co-workers and random strangers. That would be weird.

3. Being generous and giving gifts will also increase your oxytocin. And the gift does not have to be significant. I love the pay-it-forward loops that will sometimes happen at Starbucks or other fast-food restaurants. It just makes you feel warm and fuzzy all over!

Endorphins

And lastly, we have the doctor: our endorphins. Endorphins are our body's natural analgesics. When our endorphins are surging, we will experience euphoria and even have a second wind. You may have heard of the not-so-mythical "runner's high." It

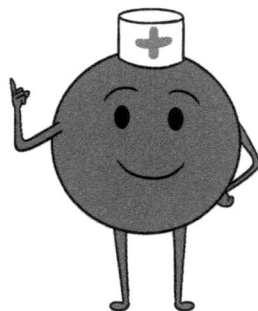

does happen, and it is thanks to the flow of endorphins. Of these four "helpers," endorphins may be the easiest to increase. And it is a triple-win: as we increase our endorphins, it is found that we also experience an increase in serotonin and dopamine!

The absence of endorphins leads to anxiety, pain, stress.

These are some excellent techniques for increasing your endorphins:

1. Laugh. Actually laugh out loud. Think about the last time you had an awesome laugh and how good it felt during and after the laugh-fest. I do not remember a lot of laughter when I was a kid, so there is one very poignant memory that I love revisiting.

    My parents were out for the evening, a few nights before Christmas. My mother was always very outspoken about her desire to receive gifts from everyone. My sister and I started feeling silly, so I joked that we should wrap up the salt and pepper shakers and put them under the tree for Mom. As we laughed about that, though, my sister added that we should wrap up the butter dish. And it continued until we pictured wrapping up everything in the kitchen, including old mail, for my mother to unwrap. We literally laughed until we were sobbing. Just thinking about that

30+-year-old memory makes me laugh to this day.

When you need a laugh, and all else fails, just Google "BBC Talking Animals." I bet you can't make it through those clips without laughing.

2. Eat. See, I told you these were easy! Specifically, eating dark chocolate and spicy foods (not necessarily at the same time) has been shown to increase endorphins.

3. Smell. Aromatherapy has also been proven effective, specifically the scents of lavender and vanilla. This can obviously vary from person to person but consider those scents that make you feel happy!

Habit #11: Identify when you have a mental and emotional shift toward negativity and take steps to hack the hijack immediately.

Workout to Make it Work Out

The ultimate way to increase your endorphins, as well as a host of other freaking fantastic things, is to exercise. Creating a consistent habit of working out will benefit your productivity in an immense proportion.

If you have ever uttered these words, "I am too busy to work out," you are full of crap. If you are too busy, that is precisely the reason you should be working out. And I do not mean that you have to do some crazy, high-intensity, extra-long workout, but commit to moving your body just 30 minutes per day. That is it. The average person spends at least three times that on their phone, scrolling through social media.

In high school, I would occasionally do aerobics (anyone remember the Jane Fonda workouts, with the awesome leotards and leg warmers? Oh, those were the days!). But as life got consumed with children and work and school, I failed to develop any type of fitness routine.

After a particularly heart-wrenching break-up, though, I did what so many people do: sought a "revenge body." I joined a gym, hired a personal trainer, and channeled my broken heart into building a stronger body. That was the first time I truly understood how powerful it was to exercise routinely, especially first thing in the morning.

To avoid the morning rush hour, I would go to the gym by my office, stupid early. The night before, I would pack my gym bag and lay out my clothes, so that there was no thinking involved. Roll out of bed, throw on some clothes, grab a cup of coffee for the ride, and head out.

I repeated this process for so long that it became a well-worn path, a habit that I no longer have even to consider. There is no alternative, competing thought. As a matter of fact, it is just the opposite. When I do not work out in the morning, I'm 'off' all day.

Benefits of exercising first thing in the morning:

- Start the day with a hit of all of those good chemicals and hormones

- You will be in a better mood at work, and you will have improvements in your concentration
- There is a pride of accomplishment that you will carry with you throughout the day
- Your blood glucose will be more in control
- You will be more inclined and inspired to eat healthier
- And ultimately, you will sleep better at night

Working out is a habit. One that can take time to build. Find something that you enjoy, but do not get turned off to it because you are uncomfortable. Remember that it is physically and physiologically impossible for us to change without some discomfort.

To keep it interesting, I mix up my workouts: Orangetheory Fitness, hiking, walking, running, cycling, and yoga. This keeps me engaged as well as it provides a better overall benefit for my body because I am challenging it in different ways.

Habit #12: Move your body for at least 30 minutes per day. Dance, walk, skip, hula hoop. Whatever you enjoy.

Emotional Intelligence

To wrap up Step Five, I am going to divulge my ultimate life-changing, career-changing epiphany: without developing your emotional intelligence, you are placing concrete limits on your life.

I am just a bit passionate about this concept of emotional intelligence. It is because I completely LACKED emotional intelligence to the point that I had an emotional intelligence intervention thrown on my ass. It was the best, most horrible, and humbling experience of my life. And I continue to be so grateful for it. Although at the time, I was traumatized and thought my career was ruined.

Emotional intelligence is the ability to understand your emotions, the impact of your emotions on others, and how to control your emotions. Once you can understand and manage your own emotions, you can then serve others: having empathy and compassion.

We learn by watching the adults around us, typically choosing to mimic their behavior. If that behavior leads to positive results, we continue to use that as a model. However, if that behavior leads to negative or detrimental impacts, ideally, we change it. But sometimes it takes an intervention or a situation for us to be aware of those negative impacts.

There was a lot of yelling in my childhood: outbursts, unpredictability, anger, bitterness, and intolerance. While I can definitively say I was not physically abused, the emotional environment certainly had an impact on me that has lasted well into my adulthood.

My parents were hot heads. I was a hot head. I had road-rage, I got angry quickly, and I was often inappropriate in my outbursts. I joked that it was just who I was. "It's in my DNA!" I claimed. To reinforce that claim, I would share the story of my dad becoming so enraged that the McDonald's drive-through was taking too long, that he threw the cup of soda through the window at the poor worker.

My Big Melt Down

The acceptability of my behavior came to a screeching halt in the middle of a corporate environment. There had been an ongoing and lingering issue between one of my teammates and me. I expected all of my peers to exhibit the same drive and work ethic that I had, and I had no tolerance for weakness or failures.

This particular team member, "Sharon," was a single mother to a challenging child. Probably in today's environment, her son would have been diagnosed as special needs. She was consistently late to meetings and would often miss work deadlines, exalting us all with the difficulties of being a single mother.

But I was also a single mother, not with one kid, but with three daughters at home. Yep. That's right. I was the one-upper gal. In my mind, I was disgusted. I was raising three kids alone and was highly dedicated to my job. And yet she only had one kid. Every time I heard, "but I'm a single mother," I wanted to be my dad in the McDonald's drive-through and throw a drink at her.

And then it happened. Well, I didn't throw a drink, but I did totally and completely freak out. I'd say I went postal, but I think that is such an insult to the fine folks that work in the U.S. postal system.

There was a meeting where I was presenting to senior leaders in the organization. A vital component of the presentation was a dashboard of all of the projects in our portfolio. Sharon was responsible for providing the underlying data. Minutes before the meeting, I realized there were errors in her data. I was going to look like a fool! I was outraged. How dare her incompetence make me look bad?

I was like a bulldog, finally let off of that short chain. I can still see her face, the shock, and what was probably terror in her eyes as I unleashed six months of pent-up frustration, anger, and bitterness at her. While I cannot remember exactly what I said, I do believe there were probably more F-bombs than any other word. This was not a quiet discussion. This was loud, messy, and absolutely horrible. In the middle of cubicle-land.

At the peak of my tirade, my boss broke it up, leading me to his office. I was still uncontrollable. He told me to leave. Go home. I was completely perplexed. Why was he sending me home and not her?

Later that day, he called and told me to come into the office in the morning. I don't think I slept the whole night. I was still so angry. In my mind, I continued to play the scene over and over again. But each time I replayed the interaction, I thought of more brilliant, and hurtful things I could have said to her.

As I was driving into the office in the morning, I prepared my speech: it is time that Sharon is fired. She is obviously disrupting our work and creating major issues. I will pick up her work, since I have practically been doing it all, anyway. Things will be so much better when she is gone.

But he did not hand Sharon a pink-slip. Instead, he gave me a plane ticket. I was confused about the plane ticket but even more confused as to why he seemed mad at me.

The plane ticket was to Minneapolis. I had two options: resign from my position or go to Minneapolis for a two-week emotional intelligence training program. I thought both options were ludicrous. How were they going to survive without me? I ran that department. I was the most critical employee. But his tone let me know he was not joking. I couldn't resign; after all, I was a *single mother*! (Oh, the irony!).

I flew up to Minneapolis, angry at the situation, angry at Sharon, angry at my boss, angry about life. It was not until a few days into the intensive program that I realized I should have been angry at myself.

And this is where my favorite quote, once again, comes into play:

"Between stimulus and response, there is a space. In that space is our power to choose our response. In our response lies our growth and our freedom." Viktor Frankl

This was the definition of emotional intelligence. I was choosing my responses. This was not Sharon's fault. This was not my boss' fault. This was not the company's fault. It was not even my parents' fault. It was 100%, entirely, totally on me. I chose my response.

Mic Drop.

Through the remainder of the class, I learned to identify my emotional triggers and the root of those triggers. Understanding my triggers allowed me to be aware of the amygdala hijack that would take place when they were present. This empowered me to break the hijack with strategies that were helpful and healthful.

Back in the office, I was a new person. Now, don't get me wrong. It did not change my triggers nor my tendencies, but it did give me the perspective to understand that I had the freedom to choose my responses.

A few months later, I returned to Minneapolis for an additional two weeks focused on understanding others' emotions, developing empathy, and building strategies to become a true, emotionally intelligent leader.

Am I perfect? No. Do I leverage these strategies still? Heck, yes, I do. Trust me, I still have those same triggers, and I must always consider my responses daily.

What does emotional intelligence have to do with productivity? Absolutely everything! We spend our day navigating through a constant barrage of emotional and physical distractions. Increased emotional intelligence allows us to navigate those distractions, choosing how and where to apply our energy.

I could write an entire book just on the impact of understanding emotional intelligence in my life. But this is not the book! I would encourage you to assess yourself and your emotional intelligence honestly. I strongly recommend any of Daniel Goleman's books on the topic.

Habit #13: Stay in touch with your emotions and your reactions to various triggers. Consider pursuing further learning about emotional intelligence.

Trigger Identification Exercise:

I want you to take a moment and consider your triggers.

1.   What are those behaviors or situations that cause you to have an emotional reaction?

_____

_____

_____

_____

_____

_____

_____

2. How do you typically respond to those triggers?

_____

_____

_____

_____

_____

3. Describe a situation where your behavior had a negative impact on yourself and/or others (and yes, this may hurt a bit):

_____

_____

_____

_____

_____

_____

4. Identify how you, your co-workers, your friends, and your family could benefit from you having better response strategies for those triggers:

_____

_____

_____

_____

_____

_____

Step Five was jam-packed with a large variety of techniques, big and small, that you can quickly implement to make significant changes in your productivity, your life, and your happiness. Do not try to do them all at once! Pick a few things to focus on, wear the path down until it becomes automatic. Once the habit is established, add on something else.

The last step in the Activation section is going to be to create an entirely new way of approaching your work and your priorities.

Key Take-Aways for Step Five:

1. Neuroplasticity allows us to create new neural pathways in our brain, which then enables us to retrain our brain.

2. Dopamine is what allows us to feel pleasure. To hack your dopamine: celebrate the small wins with incremental goals, write down your accomplishments, define what is next, eat healthily, and practice health habits.

3. Serotonin maintains our mood balance. To hack your serotonin: create a positive emotional state, get outside, meditate and re-live happy moments, eat food high in trytophans, and write in your gratitude journal.

4. Oxytocin is our love and intimacy hormone. To hack your oxytocin: give someone a handshake, share a hug with receptive partners, and give gifts.

5. Endorphins are our natural analgesic. To hack your endorphins: Laugh, eat dark chocolate and spicy foods, and use aromatherapy.

6. One of the greatest gifts you can give yourself, mentally and physically, is a consistent regimen of exercise, at least 30 minutes per day.

7. Emotional intelligence is the ability to understand your emotions and control them, while understanding and having empathy for others' emotions. Know your triggers and identify actions to employ when they are present.

Belinda Goodrich

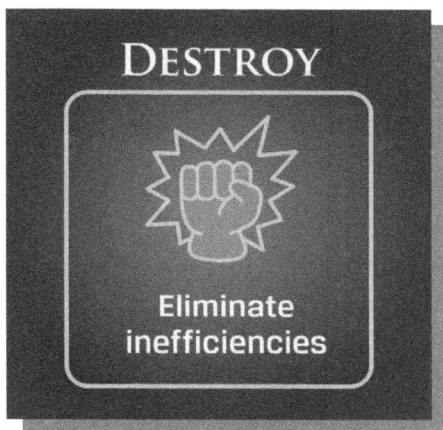

STEP 6: DESTROY

ELIMINATE INEFFICIENCIES

We are now at the last step of normalizing our productivity, and this is where the rubber hits the road. This step is all about eliminating your inefficiencies. As you begin to look at all of the places that you are putting your energy and effort during the day, you may find that what you think is making you efficient, is actually doing just the opposite. Many of us have fooled ourselves into believing that we are mastering our lives through multitasking and tools and planners. But are we?

I would request that you go into Step Six, as I have with the rest of the book, with an open mind. After all, you are reading this because you suspect perhaps there may be a better way to do things. In step six, I am going to do some significant myth-busting, especially around multitasking, the need for immediate gratification, and the use of to-do lists.

The Multitasking Fallacy

In my presentations and workshops, I will frequently ask my participants to raise their hands if they believe they are adept at multitasking and if they believe multitasking is a necessary component of productivity. At least 50% will raise their hands. If you have not yet figured this out, it is time we have a heart-to-heart talk about how damaging multitasking can be to you physically, mentally, and from a productivity perspective.

Each time we shift our attention to a new task, there is a cognitive cost. Researchers at the University of California found that the average time to refocus on a task after an interruption is 23 minutes and 15 seconds! What? Consider the incredibly damaging impact of that throughout your day.

The typical knowledge worker's office set-up could be considered a multitasking exacerbation zone:

- Computer with multiple monitors
- Email

- Multiple internet tabs
- Instant messenger
- Social media accounts
- Cell phone
- Office phone
- Co-workers
- And then the actual task that you should be focusing on

How many windows, tabs, and applications do you have open at any given time? Every time you toggle between any of these, you are paying a significant cognitive price.

New research from the University of London is finding that multitasking actually makes us dumber, dropping our IQ points down to the level of an average 8-year old child. Consider that the next time you're multitasking while writing an important email to your boss or developing a new report or deliverable.

This translates to our learning capabilities, as well. Students who are responding to social media accounts and texts while studying or doing homework have consistently lower grade point averages than those students that can stay focused.

Multitasking also negatively impacts creativity and even possibly reduces our emotional intelligence. Again, we are allowing ourselves to fully engage with the topic of our concentration long enough to give it the attention it needs.

Habit #14: Allocate blocks of time on your calendar for your focused work. Start brief and gradually increase that time. During the block, close out any internet browsers, email accounts, and turn off notifications on your phone.

Our brains are not balloons with unlimited stretchability — quite the contrary. Our attention is a very narrow and fixed pipeline that can only truly focus on one thing at a time.

Again, do not get frustrated with this as it is a function of our core survival mechanisms. If we were able to focus on multiple things, how would we easily and effectively detect a threat to our survival?

Here is the sad irony of this, though. When that focus is placed on a cell phone, with a dazzling array of distractions, we are frequently incredibly unaware of what is happening around us. Here are some staggering statistics from EndDD.org from 2016, the most current data available:

- 15% of injury crashes and 10% of fatal crashes were from distraction, but there is a belief that distracted driving crashes are significantly under-reported.

- Texting involves manual, visual, and cognitive distractions, combining all three in a highly destructive manner.

- Driving while on the cell phone is the equivalent of being intoxicated at a 0.08% blood-alcohol limit.

- Sending a text message takes your eyes off the road for 5 seconds. At 55 mph, that would cover the distance of a football field.

- Teens are much more likely to drive distracted if

> they witness their parents driving distracted.
>
> Excuse me while I step up onto a great big colossal soapbox:
>
> PUT YOUR DAMN PHONE DOWN
>
> It is not worth losing your life or someone else's. There is nothing that urgent. And if it is, pull over.
>
> *Stepping off of my soapbox now.*

Immediate Gratification

In Step Five, I discussed dopamine. Remember, this is our feel-good hormone that is often involved in addiction cycles. While it certainly can be useful and positive, there is a disturbing trend that researchers are seeing. We are now living in an immediate world full of distractions.

As we habitually get distracted, such as checking our cell phones first thing in the morning, constantly checking our email, or scrolling through our social media accounts, we have actually trained our brains to lose focus. We have worn that neural pathway so well, in fact, that we do not even have to consciously think about picking up our phone or shifting from one stimulus to the other.

So much so, according to Daniel Levitin, a neuroscientist, that we are creating a "dopamine-addiction feedback loop, effectively rewarding the brain for losing focus and for constantly searching for external stimulation." We are immediate gratification junkies —

distraction – dopamine, distraction – dopamine, distraction – dopamine.

Just to be clear, we are experiencing a dopamine high each time we lose focus. Holy crap. Do you see how much damage this is causing us, and how much it is hurting our productivity? We actually *crave* distractions just as a junkie craves their next shot of heroin.

How addicted are you to distractions?

Distraction Addiction Exercise:

Commit to a 48-hour evaluation of your distraction addiction level.

- Set a stopwatch on your phone or write down the current time that is showing on your clock.

- Begin working on a task.

- Stop the clock when your focus shifts to something else: an email, a text message, or something other than your intended focus.

- Keep a record of the time between each reallocation of your focus.

- At the end of the 48-hours, calculate the average amount of time you were able to devote to a task.

- Use these results as a benchmark to allow yourself to improve.

- Set an improvement goal.

- Repeat the exercise, monitoring your progress against your goal.

Destroy the To-Do List. Really.

As a young adult, I remember going to see Jack Agati speak in Boston. He was a well-known presenter on the topic of birth order. He asked how many of us like to make lists. I eagerly raised my hand. Then he asked how many of us, when we do something that was not on our list, add it to our list after the fact so that we can cross it off. Again, my hand shot up. Oh, yes, I love my lists!

I am an incredibly visual person, and I am completely infatuated with creating lists. I even have lists of my lists. Imagine my shock and dismay when I learned that while many lists are great (such as a shopping list, written in order of the departments of the grocery store), to-do lists can be very harmful to our productivity. Say it ain't so!

Picture it. You have gotten yourself organized, identified your priorities, and have created a glorious, comprehensive to-do list. It is truly a work of art. Maybe you have even color-coded it! How can this incredible instrument of productivity be anything but good? You see all your tasks, and as you get them done, you cross it off. Ahhh! Sweet satisfaction. Nothing beats crossing something off from your to-do list.

But there's a big problem hiding just beneath the joyous celebration of crossing an item off the list. While we may receive a momentary feeling of satisfaction upon boldly striking through the completed item, nanoseconds later, your subconscious brain pulls a hijack.

On average, people will have 15 to 20 things on their to-do list. In a typical day, many folks will complete four or five of those items and maybe add one or two.

Your conscious brain, says, "woohoo, you rocked it out!" exalting on what you crossed off the list.

The subconscious brain, however, is a simpleton. It evaluates our environments based on a series of comparisons. It is incredibly literal. In looking at that to-do list, your subconscious brain does not celebrate what you have completed. Instead, it sends a stress signal to the limbic system because it is looking at what has *not* been done.

Again, a system of comparison: you completed probably less than 25% of what was your list. It is not happy for the 25%, it is stressed over the remaining 75%. The subconscious focuses on the negative.

Your limbic system gets the "Oh no, we are overwhelmed" message, gives you a negative hit of cortisol (the stress hormone), and your temporary joy you received from the conscious brain moves to the background and the subconscious feedback now overwrites it.

You do not even realize that this is happening. But maybe you suddenly feel a little down, perhaps a little frustrated, and possibly overwhelmed. And your dear little conscious brain has no idea why.

I believe our obsession with to-do lists and planners is one of the reasons many people are discouraged and frustrated in today's work environment. This makes work not fun. In fact, it makes it suck. So apologies right now if you just went out and bought that fancy planner to get yourself organized.

But do not burn it just yet, because we can use it productively by putting it in a vault!

The Vault Strategy

The magic number for human engagement and focus is seven plus or minus two. Again, like the Law of Attraction, this is just a universal known. Five to nine items. That is what our brain can effectively handle.

You will notice there are nine steps in the GET IT DONE process. This was not an accident!

Using a vault strategy keeps you on-point and focused while leveraging a nice hack of those happy juices we discussed in Step Five.

1. Write down your top priorities for the week

2. Validate that those priorities align with your life goals and mission that you defined in Step One

3. For the highest priority item, break the work down into microbites: small, incremental pieces of work that are ideally able to be completed in four hours or less

4. Write each of those microbites on a sticky note

5. Lock your big list away "in a vault," somewhere out of sight

6. Stick the first sticky note to your computer or workspace somewhere where you can see it (the other sticky notes are stacked up nearby)

7. Create your uninterruptable cocoon (shut off the phone, email, etc.)

8. Focus only on that first microbite until it is completed

9. Upon finishing, grab that sticky note off of your workspace, crumple it up and throw it in the trash

10. Your conscious and subconscious brain are in gorgeous, productive harmony at this moment, agreeing that you are the most incredibly productive and awesome person in the world

11. Bathe in the splash of dopamine, serotonin, and endorphins that you are being rewarded with at this moment

12. Grab your next sticky note and get to work

13. Repeat this process until all of the microbites associated with that priority are done, and now you can unlock your vault

14. Pull out your big list and assess your next priority item and approach it in the same microbite fashion

If you follow this process, I promise you it will work, and it will feel so good! Now, I cannot wholly take the credit for this because I stumbled upon it a little bit by accident through my career as a project manager.

Habit #15: Do not keep a long to-do list visible to you throughout the workday. Focus on microbites, small tasks, completing one at a time.

Being Agile

Without boring you with all of the details, it was the introduction of agile project management that opened my eyes to core human productivity alignment. Unlike traditional, or waterfall, project management where we plan the work and work the plan, in agile project management, we have a list of requirements, but the team only focuses on small pieces of work during a set time increment.

Team members leverage tools to limit the work-in-progress, such as burn-down charts (to visually see their progress) or a Kanban board. The idea behind agile is that team members should work at a healthy, sustainable pace. They focus on only one task at a time and are not continually looking at all of the future work.

While agile approaches are not appropriate for all project environments, the underlying concepts are incredibly powerful for individual productivity: a visual representation of the work, singular focus on one task until it is completed, the ability to reprioritize easily between increments of work.

In the project world, when agile is executed as intended, team members and customers realize higher quality and satisfaction, reduced costs, and focused sustainability.

Retrospectives and Daily Stand-Ups

In traditional project management, we are expected to conduct a final review of how the project went, evaluating our successes and failures. These sessions were called post-implementation reviews, post-mortems, etc. The problem is that no one cares once the project is done, and very rarely did these sessions elicit ground-breaking information or learnings.

With agile project management, the team evaluates their work and environment at the end of every increment or sprint of work. For most agile teams, the increments are two to four weeks in length. In the retrospective, the team identifies what is working well, what is not working so well, and what they can adapt or adjust to make improvements. This is genius! The idea of a set and scheduled time allocation to evaluate how to get better. And then they actually implement those positive actions to improve continuously.

I do not want you to wait for two to four weeks, especially as you just begin on this program of improved productivity and fulfillment. I want you to conduct a retrospective each day diligently. It is hugely valuable and relatively easy:

1. Start your day with a vision of how the day is going to progress and your critical priorities for the day (thinking in the positive!)

2. Practice some of the GET IT DONE habits

3. End the day with an evaluation: What worked? What didn't? How can you tweak it and improve it for tomorrow?

4. Start the next day with any identified tweaks

5. Recognize that you can always get better, and you can continually improve!

Habit #16: Conduct your personal retrospective in *writing*. Yes, actually handwrite it in a journal or notebook. The act of handwriting actually helps us create those new neural pathways I have been talking about throughout this book. When you handwrite the good things that are happening and those that you are going to change, you are literally writing them onto your brain and into existence.

Another powerful technique that I borrow from agile project management is doing a daily stand-up. As a replacement for your typical weekly status meeting, the daily stand-up is precisely what it sounds like it is. Team members stand up and report their status:

- What they did the previous workday
- What they are doing today
- Any challenges or obstacles that they are facing

The idea of them standing is to prevent anyone from getting too comfortable and talking longer than necessary. These daily stand-ups are limited to 15 minutes and are strictly for status reporting, not problem-solving.

I do these daily stand-ups with my team but also apply these concepts to myself personally. I am acknowledging what I accomplished yesterday (surge of endorphins and dopamine) and what I plan to accomplish today (a hit of adrenaline). This helps me reap the positive benefits of student syndrome: putting things off until the last minute.

Because I know that I will be reporting on my progress in 24 hours, it is time to get it done. I am putting myself in a position to experience some positive stress – the appropriate amount of adrenaline and cortisol to actively engage me in ensuring that work gets done. The shorter the accountability period, the higher the likelihood is that the task will get the focus it needs.

Habit #17: At the start of each workday, increase your gratitude and accountability by acknowledging what you accomplished the previous day and what you will achieve during the current day.

Putting This Into Action

This is perhaps one of the most exacting steps of the GET IT DONE process. I am challenging you to rewire some habits that have become wholly engrained in your subconscious to the point that you do not even realize that they are happening. And you perhaps, do not even realize the damage that they are causing. This step takes diligent and consistent effort and practice. It is not going to happen overnight, so please give yourself some grace. Baby steps are better than no steps.

With all of my heart, I guarantee you that if you give these things the proper focus, you will witness a change in you as a person. You will be more productive, and ultimately, you will be happier and more at ease. Remember, change is uncomfortable. But I have faith in you, and I know you can do it.

Key Take-Aways from Step Six:

1. You are not good at multitasking. No one is. If you think you are, I am here to tell you, you are not. Sorry.

2. Multitasking robs us of cognitive functioning, creativity, emotional intelligence, and lowers our IQ.

3. Put your damn phone down when you are driving.

4. We have become addicted to distractions. We are literally distraction-junkies that feed on the release of dopamine when we get distracted.

5. The to-do list needs to be replaced with microbites of work.

6. You will work on one microbite at a time before tackling the next microbite.

7. You can only unlock the vault holding your to-do list when your current microbites are completed. At that time, you are welcome to reprioritize what is remaining on your list.

8. Conducting daily retrospectives, in writing, allows you to make adjustments to fine-tune your work and your prioritization approach.

9. Daily stand-ups create healthy tension and stress to engage us in getting the highest priority work completed in a timely fashion.

You are now 2/3 of the way through the GET IT DONE process. In your final section, you will work on normalizing what it is you have learned, constantly reinforcing those neural pathways.

Congratulations! The hard work is done. It is time just to put the cherry on top!

Section 3

Normalize

Steps 7 - 9

Belinda Goodrich

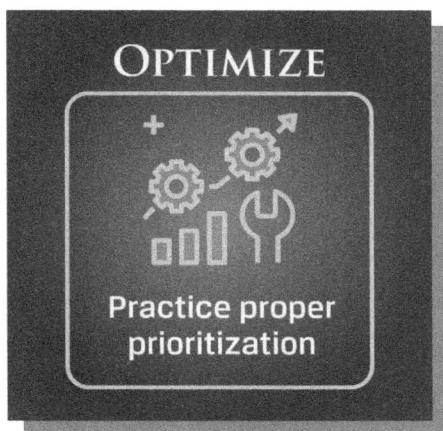

STEP 7: OPTIMIZE

PRACTICE PROPER PRIORITIZATION

Normalizing is all about settling into positive routines with the new techniques and habits that you have learned and are practicing. I am going to challenge you in this section to move beyond just getting more done but to genuinely finding joy in your life. I want you to jump out of bed every single day, excited about what you have ahead of you, versus dreading what is happening to you. Attack the day like a shark!

Belinda Goodrich

What We Prioritize by Not Prioritizing

I remember the day as if it was yesterday. I was taking care of my youngest granddaughter, Cadence, while her mother, my daughter, was attending her college class. It had been a long day, and I had a list of things to get through that night. I was tired and probably more than a bit cranky.

Cadence came up to me with a plastic taco and said, "c'mon Grammy, play food truck with me!" her little hand grabbing mine and pulling me towards the living room. And away from the dishes I was about to do.

"Grammy has some things to…..," but before I could finish the statement, I remember what I had recently advised my audience members to do:

When someone or something is trying to get your attention, and you are choosing to do something different (such as checking your cell phone, answering an email, or doing the dishes) give yourself an honest gut-check by saying, *out loud* "I'm sorry <insert name>, but I am choosing to prioritize <my cell phone, my email, doing the dishes> over you."

What a reality check and not a pleasant one. But I took my own advice. I looked down at that sweet little face, still dirty from a busy day at daycare, hair scraggly (looking a bit like Joe Dirt), and I said, "I'm sorry, Cadence. Grammy is prioritizing doing dishes over spending some time playing with you." The words made my heart hurt, but even more painful was the disappointed look in her eyes.

"You know what?" I said, "I think the dishes can wait. What do you have in your food truck?" A smile bounced across her face, and she eagerly pulled me toward the Fisher-Price food truck tucked in the corner of the living room. For the next hour, she treated me to plastic tacos, burgers, and expertly created pretend smoothies. She counted out change and grilled the food as if there was nothing more in the world that she would want to do. I think that hour may have been more fun for her than our trip to Disneyland earlier in the year. And truth be told, I was having fun, too.

Now, does that mean that we can just turn our backs on the un-fun stuff in life? Absolutely not! Don't be a slob. Do your dishes, make your bed, file your taxes. All of that unglamorous stuff. But do it with a purpose and with the appropriate prioritization.

The grandkids know that I make my bed every day. They don't see it as competing with their time with me, because we do it together, usually while singing "Did You Feed My Cow?". This little silly act has created a memorable experience for both them and me in the mornings after a sleepover, and they are learning that household duties can still be fun.

> Habit #18: Verbalize, yes out loud, that you are prioritizing whatever it is you are doing over another task or action that you believe you probably should be doing. That verbal acknowledgment may be enough to shift your attention and encourage you to make a different choice.

My best friend and I recently took a trip to Epcot Center. Which, by the way, was a lot of fun when it is just adults and no kids! We were standing in the line for a ride, and as I looked around, I was dismayed at what I saw because it was similar to what I had witnessed in the airport. And we were at The Happiest Place on Earth!

What should have been excellent family bonding time with excited parents and children was much more commonly cellphone time. Parents with their heads bent at an angle wrapped up in whatever was on their phone. Teenagers were absorbed in their screens. Little children were pulling on their parents, desperately trying to get their attention. It sincerely broke my heart. How much money had these families invested in taking this trip, and yet here is how they were spending that time?

I thought about how that experience differed from when my children were young, long before cell phones, and my focus was entirely on them. I am so grateful, now, that I did not have a cell phone tearing me away from my kids.

My girls, all grown up now, and I were talking recently about their best memories of childhood. Like a lot of parents, I struggled with mom-guilt, wishing I could have provided more for them. They grew up knowing we were living paycheck-to-paycheck during their younger years. I was surprised and incredibly touched when they all agreed on their best memory:

On Friday nights after I finished work, we would get in the car and drive to the shopping mall on the complete opposite side of the city. Along the way, we would crank up Melissa Etheridge and sing at the top of our lungs. Horribly off-key, but off-key together, so it was ok!

At the mall, we would walk around, looking at the cool things and people-watching. The only thing they were able to buy was a candy necklace from the candy store. And that was perfectly ok. I would take them out to dinner, and we would talk about their week and sometimes just act silly. Such as the night we all decided we should change our last names: Brandie Candy, Brookie Cookie, and Brittany Pick-Up Truck. (It was hard to come up with something that rhymed with *Brittany*).

I love those memories. And I am so incredibly grateful that I did not have a phone. My memories are not clouded with me focusing on a screen instead of their sweet faces. It is the perfect reminder for me to be present with my grandchildren and all of the people in my life now that cell phones are a constant temptation.

I challenge you to become acutely aware of these moments and what you are prioritizing by not prioritizing. At your next family or friends gathering, request it to be a non-phone event, encouraging engagement and discussion.

And bring this idea outside of your personal gatherings. Nothing makes a person feel completely invisible, less-than, or unworthy than when a customer is too busy on their phone to acknowledge them. I love to study people, and I watch facial expressions of the parties during different transactions. More frequently than not, a look of hurt and sometimes even embarrassment will cross the face of the worker when their customer does not take the time to acknowledge and engage with them because they are too busy on their phone.

Flip that transaction around, however, and the difference is incredible. Talk to your uber driver, your waiter or bartender, the courtesy clerk, or anyone else that is serving you. Ask them how their day is going or ask them, "so what's good in your world today?". It is amazing how quickly most people will brighten up and enjoy the chatter about happy things.

Remember what is occurring under the surface during this transaction when you engage in joyful conversation: You are getting a shot of oxytocin because you have *connected* with someone. They are also the lucky recipients of some oxytocin, and also serotonin. You have brought them to a place where they are focusing on something positive. What an incredible gift!

I like to say that people are either purposely rude or ignorantly rude. Because we thrive in this world of insanity and distractions, I would like to believe that most of us are ignorantly rude, that we genuinely have no idea how our behavior is impacting those around us. But as you have gone through the GET IT DONE process, you are growing your self-awareness. Which, in turn, will allow you to be more insightful as to how your behavior is not only impacting you but impacting those around you.

Hint #19: During transactions, put your phone aside and actually talk to the person taking care of you, smile, and say thank you. And put your cart in the cart corral when you are done shopping. #Karma

---

Consciously Guiding Your Behavior

"Would the person you want to be, be doing what you are doing right now?"

I challenged you with this earlier in the book. Now that you are putting all of the GET IT DONE steps into practice, continually ask yourself this question. It will allow you to course-correct and bring you back into alignment with your goals.

Life does not happen to you. You are not a bystander, an observer. You are in control, and that control comes through your choices. To gain some success and traction on these productivity habits, I recommend using habit clustering.

In habit clustering or grouping, you identify a set of habits that you want to ritualize and practice, and you do them all together as one set block. For example, my morning routine is the same: I make my bed, do my workout, and do my daily plan and prioritization. In the evening, I write my daily retrospective, write in my gratitude journal, and meditate before going to bed.

By clustering or grouping your habits, they start to reinforce the others. It seems weird or off to me, now, to do my workout if I have not yet made my bed. I have it so deeply programmed in my subconscious as a set group and pattern, that it is challenging to separate them. They have become linked as one set habit.

I recommend the following habit clusters:

- Morning routine (exercise, planning, self-care, etc.)
- Productivity cocoon routine (eliminate distractions, create an environment of productivity, etc.) when you start work
- Social engagement routine (put the phone away, smile, talk to people, etc.)
- Bedtime routine (journal, retrospective, plan for the next day, etc.)

Our brain thrives in homeostatic environments, so by creating these predictable patterns of positive actions, we are allowing for and nurturing that homeostasis. It is no less essential for us as adults to have routines as it is for our children to have routines. When we know what to expect, it eliminates the stress associated with the unknowns. The challenge is simply to overwrite negative routines with positive routines.

Improving Your Focus

I am going to let you in on my biggest productivity secret. But I will honestly admit, I did not create it. It is known as the Pomodoro Technique, and Francesco Cirillo developed it in the late 1980s. It is so named for the tomato-shaped timer he used to track his time.

The Pomodoro Technique was brought to my attention when I joined a writing group. They were using a chunking approach to the two-hour meeting. I just thought they had randomly created the structure. But it was actually routed in neuropsychology.

In the writing group, we would all join the meeting virtually using Zoom, with our cameras on us. For the first five minutes, we would share what we were working on during the session and what our goals were. At the 5-minute mark, participants place themselves on mute and write for 25 minutes.

An alarm goes off from the moderator, signaling that the 25 minutes is complete. For the next five minutes, we share any concerns, questions, or challenges. And then start back up again for the next 25-minute block. This is repeated four times during the two-hour session. That is 100 minutes of dedicated productivity in a 120-minute block.

It was through these meetings and this process that I was able to complete my book *Kick Ass Project Manager* very quickly. I could not believe the increase in my productivity. So, of course, being me, I had to dissect it and really understand what was happening and why.

I recognized a few of the immediate benefits:

- The two-hour meeting was blocked out on my calendar, thus eliminating competing events.
- The fact that I had RSVP'd to attend the session increased

my likelihood of attending. I had now committed to being there.

- My camera being on was another accountability measure. If I picked up my phone and started scrolling through Facebook, my peers would see that.

- By sharing my goals with the group, I was making my book a reality.

- The block of time was the perfect amount of time to sit and focus. I could do anything for 25 minutes. And I could undoubtedly block out two hours of my day twice per week. Not too long. Not too short.

It was after finishing *Kick Ass Project Manager* and beginning to use this structure for other vital tasks, that I learned it was actually a thing, known as the Pomodoro Technique. Essentially, your workday is structured using two-hour blocks, with a five-minute break after every 25-minute increment of work. At the end of the two-hour block you take a 20-minute break before starting the next block.

Ideally, that 20-minute break should be spent doing something active. Stretching, walking, or something that gets you moving.

Using the Pomodoro technique is strengthening your brain to focus during defined periods of time. This is one of the most compelling methods for breaking that distraction-addiction discussed earlier.

Habit #20: Break up your workday into 2-hour chunks of work, using the 25/5 system. Set a timer and close off any distractions. If you have a peer or co-worker on the same schedule, consider creating an accountability partnership with them, using the same system.

Banish Meetings

At one point in my corporate career, I had several project managers on my team. As part of their professional development, I would ask them to read *Death by Meeting* by Pat Lencioni. Most would greet the request with a laugh or a smirk. "Isn't that what we experience every day?"

And it was true, which is why I had them read the book. Inefficient and inappropriate meetings are killing our productivity.

Chris was exhausted. He glanced down at his phone and realized it was 7 p.m. And there he was, still in his office. This was now becoming the norm since taking on his new role as a director.

His calendar was completely out-of-control, with meetings scheduled throughout the day from 8 a.m. until 5 p.m. Of course, with each meeting, he would walk away with a list of action items. The only opportunity he had actually to get that work done, was early in the morning before anyone else was in the office or in the evening after everyone had left.

But he was realizing the toll that it was taking on him and his family. He recently had to miss his son's band concert and his daughter's volleyball game. It was time for a change.

Does this sound familiar to you? If you are a knowledge worker, in a corporate setting, you may have found yourself trapped into this detrimental cycle of having to work before and after work hours because meetings have consumed the regular workday. The more senior you get in your career, the more likely this is to happen.

The average office worker spends over 31 hours per month in unproductive meetings, according to Atlassian. Thirty-one hours per month. Just think about how much more we could be getting done if we could take back that time.

Truthfully, many of the meetings that are scheduled are not legitimate. Be the bulldog on that short chain, and viciously protect your schedule and your calendar. Before allowing any meeting requests to come in, block out your dedicated work times on your calendar. If the time is showing as available, it will be too easy to accept requests as they come in. Lock that shit down.

Parkinson's Law states that work will expand so as to consume the time allocated to it. I see this play out over and over in corporate meetings. There is an hour scheduled for the meeting, so it takes an hour. But did it really need to take an hour? Probably not.

Strategies to End Productivity Death by Meeting

- Adjust your meetings to be in shorter time increments. For example, consider changing a typically one-hour meeting to start at 15 minutes after the hour and run it for 45 minutes or even 30 minutes.

- Create and strictly enforce meeting ground rules. Ground rules could include starting and stopping the meeting on time, sticking to the agenda, and ending the meeting when objectives are met versus consuming the entire time allocation.

- If it is your meeting, distribute the agenda to the participants ahead of time, including clearly defining the expectations of the participants. This will minimize confusion and additional discussion during the actual meeting.

- Scrutinize any meeting request that you get. Does it serve a purpose? Is there a quicker way to handle the discussion (a phone call, an email)? Is it a priority for you to attend?

- Change your weekly status meeting to a daily stand-up meeting, as discussed previously. If you really want to up your game, make participants hold out a ream of paper as they are reporting their status. It is amazing how heavy that paper gets. Brevity is queen!

- Have a no-phone rule during your meetings. Keep everyone focused on the agenda and the topics.

- If it is feasible, make the meeting mobile! Take a walk during your discussions, giving yourself some endorphins from exercise, while working through the topics. My best team meetings happen on the hiking trail!

Habit #21: Control your calendar proactively, not allowing your calendar to control you. Eliminate unnecessary meetings. Block your work time first.

Productive Multitasking

I know, I know. I have completely beat you up on how evil multitasking is and given you horror stories as to the damage it is causing. But I want to conclude Step Seven with some ideas around productive multitasking.

The idea with productive multitasking is that you partner

something up that is autonomic and somewhat boring (able to run efficiently in the background) with something that requires more focus.

Essentially, I want you to examine the hours of your day where you are doing something rather automatically with minimal thought and focus. The most common example is your daily commute. How much time do you spend in your car or on public transportation? How do you use that time?

This is the ideal time to learn! I am a major bibliophile, and I much prefer hardcopy print books than Kindle or Audible versions; however, I am now in the pattern of purchasing a good percentage of my books on Audible. This is deliberate so that I can hear them while I'm commuting or doing other tasks.

I love music, and that was my typical go-to choice. But I was lamenting about how I never have time to read and needed to change my perspective from *lack* to *how can I?* When I thoroughly examined my calendar, I found multiple pockets of time where I could, indeed, be listening to these books. I had been so focused on my lack of time to read that I did not, at first, consider how I could gain the knowledge within the books.

But it is not only books that can enrich you. We are a burgeoning podcast society, as well. Find podcasts that are educational, inspirational, and motivational. That direct auditory impact is incredible! It is like you are literally planting positivity seeds in your brain.

To really increase your absorption game, listen to your book or podcast when you are walking, running, or hiking. This will provide multiple benefits: your workouts will go much quicker, you are partnering up endorphins, serotonin, and dopamine (especially when you are outside), and you are gaining knowledge and inspiration while getting healthier.

My team always knows to expect a brilliant list of ideas when I come off of the trail, having listened to a book or podcast during my hike. As soon as I get into my car, I jot down these ideas and throw them into the hopper for prioritization.

This type of productive multitasking can take place anytime you are on autopilot: driving, exercising, cleaning the house, taking a shower, or tending to errands. Become a growth-junkie by layering on new ideas with tasks that you typically do not enjoy. I find that I actually look forward to doing a power-clean on my house because I will be learning as I'm cleaning!

Habit #22: Use the time you devote to rote tasks to productively multitask.

Key Take-Aways from Step Seven:

1. Become very consciously aware of what you are prioritizing by not prioritizing

2. When choosing to avert your attention from someone or something, call yourself out on it verbally

3. Be kind to and engage service workers: smile, have a conversation, remember your manners

4. Cluster sets of habits into multiple blocks throughout your day

5. Use a Pomodoro Technique or something similar to chunk out your focus time

6. Kill unproductive meetings

7. Practice productive multitasking, overlaying autonomic tasks with something stimulating

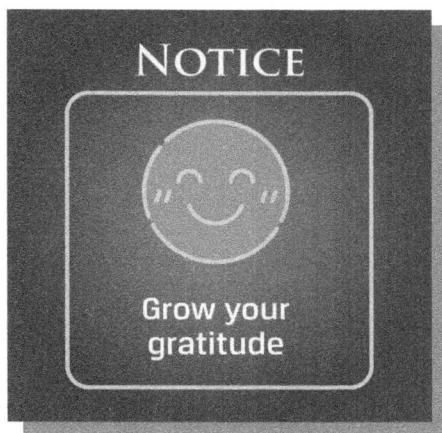

NOTICE

Grow your
gratitude

STEP 8: NOTICE

GROW YOUR GRATITUDE

Throughout this book, I have challenged you that the GET IT DONE process is not merely about getting more done in the hours we have available to us. Instead, it is about getting more of the right things done to have a harmonious and fulfilled life. You deserve to live a happy life. And you are entirely in control of living a life of joy. And joy is a by-product of living a life of gratitude.

In Step Eight, I am moving you away from tactical actions and engaging your mind to retrain your subconscious.

Rewire for Positivity

Neuropsychologists recognize that our brains are wired to focus on negative events. Consider when you were in school, and you brought home your report card. If you were like many others, the focus was on the areas of deficiency. Maybe that was from you, or perhaps it was from your parents, or maybe it was both.

From a young age, we are trained to focus on negative things, and again this simply is attributable to the survival of our species.

However, we have learned throughout GET IT DONE that you can rewire your brain with new habits. This is going to be the key ingredient in creating a life of joy and abundance. I am going to give you multiple techniques to develop new practices that will retrain your brain to focus on the positives, eliminating or minimizing the focus on the negatives.

A few years ago, I was delivering the closing keynote to an audience of about 500 project managers. I was so proud of the fact that I was selected to close out the program, and I was incredibly diligent in creating a presentation that the audience would find beneficial. They were my peers, and with over twenty years as a corporate project manager, I felt I understood their challenges.

I delivered my keynote, and throughout the presentation, the audience was engaged and receptive. I stepped off that stage feeling like I had given them everything I had in me. It felt awesome.

A few weeks later, the conference coordinator sent me the feedback from the participants, complimenting me on the incredibly high score and excellent comments from the audience. I opened the spreadsheet and sorted it by satisfaction score. Without even thinking about, I immediately scrolled to the bottom, the lowest scores. With my heart beating loudly inside of my chest, I read the two negative comments. I felt like I had been stabbed in the gut.

The most painful part of their comments was that what they stated I believed to be utterly untrue in my heart of hearts. They had assessed a judgment against me that was hurtful and embarrassing, all from a 45-minute keynote presentation.

I started questioning if I should be a professional speaker, after all. Why would I put myself out there for so much hurtful criticism? Maybe I wasn't any good. Perhaps I didn't know what I was talking about. Maybe I was stupid. Maybe, maybe, maybe. And it was even more devastating because I had thought I had done so well. How could I have misread the audience?

This experience shook my world for a lot longer than I care to admit. And even now, putting it into writing, those same feelings of shame, worthlessness, and embarrassment, come back. I finally realized the detriment of these feelings and had to dissociate myself from the situation and look at it as an impartial observer.

First of all, there were 500 people in that audience. Two people chose to write something hurtful. Two people. I was letting and allowing the negative words of two people to prevent me from helping and serving however many others. I owned my response to that stimulus, and my response was wrong.

I later learned that many speakers struggle with this and have found that those that have been in the industry for an extended period eliminate the "bottom of the bucket" feedback from their consideration. It is just a given assumption that there will always be people who do not like you. You cannot control that.

In her book *Girl, Wash Your Face*, Rachel Hollis talks about reading her book reviews. She was utterly devastated over how hateful some of the reviews were towards her. She decided, at that point, to stop reading the reviews. It served her no purpose to agonize over why some people did not like her.

But again, you can see as humans, we tend to gravitate to the negative. Now, by all means, I am not saying we should not seek out constructive feedback. That is a significant hallmark of high emotional intelligence when you can process negative feedback and react reasonably. But we must not allow that negative feedback to create a harmful overreaction.

To rewire for positivity, we must genuinely stop and smell the flowers. It reminds me of one of my favorite childhood stories *Ferdinand the Bull*. He simply loved smelling the flowers in the field. I went back to the feedback and, for the first time, read all of the positive comments. It made me glow!

Be Ferdinand. Notice the positive things around you. And I do not mean just give them a passing glance. Truly stop and give your undivided attention to that thing for 20 to 30 seconds. Just soak in all that goodness.

Habit #23: When you see something that makes you happy, stop everything else, and allow yourself to focus on it for 20 to 30 seconds.

As we sat on those chairs, looking out over the lake, my best friend and I were genuinely immersing ourselves in the beauty that we were seeing. That is why, at that moment, amidst all the turmoil and crap, we were able to be just truly and blissfully happy. When I am in New England, especially in the autumn, it is not unusual for me to pull off on the side of the road and see the beauty of the trees and nature around me.

This is the practice of mindfulness. If we have ever needed to learn mindfulness in the history of man and woman, this is the time. When we slow down and focus just on the present moment and our breathing, our stress decreases, and the level of cortisol (the stress hormone) in our bloodstream is reduced.

When mindfulness is practiced regularly, an amazing phenomenon occurs within our prefrontal cortex (our logical brain). Gyrification, which is the formation of more folds in our brain, occurs, allowing us to improve all of those higher functioning tasks, such as thinking creatively, making reasonable decisions, and creating flexibility.

Practice Gratitude

Having a life of joy means genuinely being grateful for what you have versus putting your thoughts and energy on what you are lacking. The best way to create a habit of gratitude is by practicing it daily. Start your day by writing down three things you are grateful for that day, repeating the exercise before you go to bed (trying not to repeat the same items for at least a month!).

As you begin reliving these things each morning and each evening, your brain and your body is swimming in happy juice! As we mentioned in hacking the hijack, the brain reacts the same way to a happy memory as it does to a pleasant real-time situation. By reliving those happy memories, we experience a nice boost of dopamine and oxytocin.

Another way to practice gratitude is to express your appreciation! Tell people how grateful you are for them or what they are doing for you. Whenever you feel you need to apologize to someone, always partner it with your gratitude.

"I am sorry I am late. Thank you so much for waiting for me patiently."

An apology without gratitude is relatively hollow. Make sure the people around you know how much you appreciate them.

The Power of Affirmations

The pure, hard truth is that negative thoughts and self-talk become self-fulfilling prophecies. The universal Law of Attraction tells us that where we put our thoughts and our energy is what will result. If you think you are fat, you will be fat. If you think you are dumb, you will be dumb. If you believe you are no good at relationships, you will be no good at relationships.

But using affirmations is not just about how you look or your personal life.

This Law of Attraction is one of the most critical aspects of changing our work and life habits that influence our productivity. Many of us have settled into a pattern of being overwhelmed, overworked, frustrated, tired, and pleading for more hours in the day. It has now truly become a self-fulfilling prophecy.

If you look at a list of tasks and think, "I will never be able to get it all done!". Guess what? You will never get it done.

I have learned to incorporate a consistent flow of positive self-talk in my life. This has been truly transformative, for example, when it comes to my running.

Here was my original script:

"Oh, God, I hate running. Why do I have to run? How come I gain weight so easy? If I were skinny, I wouldn't have to run. Do people really enjoy this, because I think this sucks? I am not an athlete. My body is not made to run. I am sturdy Maine stock, not a damn gazelle. My lungs hurt. My lungs cannot handle running. My feet hurt. My back hurts. I can't breathe. Am I done yet? My GPS must be wrong, I have run at least six miles, not .2 of a mile." And so on.

I flipped my script when I became incredibly mindful of my self-talk.

Now my script goes like this:

"My legs are strong. I am so proud of my muscle memory. Look at the pretty sunrise. I am so grateful I get to be outdoors. I feel so good. My breathing is great. Thank you, legs, for carrying me down this road. Thank you, lungs, for giving me fresh air. I am a freaking running rock star! I love to run! I feel amazing!".

And yes, this is literally my script. As soon as a negative thought comes knocking at the door, I completely squash it and replace it with a positive affirmation. Once I flipped my script, my running became more enjoyable, and I stopped having the injuries, aches, and pains. I was more consistent with my pace, and I found myself not dreading the miles ahead of me.

In the movie The Help, nanny Aibileen Clack whispers to her young charge, "You is Kind. You is Smart. You is Important." Powerful messages to that little girl. In 1991, Stuart Smalley was a character on Saturday Night Live that would offer "Daily Affirmations with Stuart Smalley." It seemed silly at the time I first watched it, but now I recognize the power of those affirmations.

My friend, you need to be gentle with yourself. Talk to yourself in the way that you deserve to be talked to and teach those around you, especially our children, to do the same.

And your affirmations have the power to set the entire tone of the day. Before you even get out of bed, start the day by creating your positive intention. Visualize how freaking awesome your day is going to be. See yourself being successful, productive, and happy at the end of the day. Create the day you want to have before your feet even touch the floor.

Meditation

In Step Two, I shared the power of meditation. As you practice mindfulness, self-love, and affirmations, you will recognize more and more how meditation can contribute to all of those.

In this chaotic world, you deserve to take at least 15 minutes a day, just for yourself. Give yourself the gift of that time to be mindful of your breathing. Practice self-love and create your affirmations while you are meditating. This is not fluffy new-age bullshit. This is literally, physiologically changing your brain, and it is much more potent than any prescription drug on the market.

The Healing Power of Mother Nature

There is no doubt I am an outdoorsy gal. There is no place you can put me on this earth that feels as good as just being out in the woods or out on the trail. I am incredibly grateful that I did not have to create that as a habit. It was thoroughly ingrained in me from birth. This was innate and not taught, as my mother and stepfather were the furthest thing from loving the outdoors.

I liked animals better than people, and I found joy in all of the creatures of the forest, including snakes and skunks and any others that had a bad rep. I once spent four hours trying to unstick a little lizard from a horrid sticky trap that our exterminator had put in our garage without my knowledge. (For the record, he survived minus his tail).

Later in life, I came to learn all of the incredible scientific benefits of spending time outside: being outside for 20 minutes gives you energy comparable to a cup of coffee, it improves our vision, boosts our immune system, and provides a source of aromatherapy.

Not to mention that the sunlight gives us a dose of vitamin D, increases our serotonin, and may help ward off depression and frustration. Being outside also increases our likelihood of exercising, improving our stamina and energy for the exercise. I can attest to this when I compare a run on a treadmill versus a run under the beautiful sky!

There are many illnesses associated with increased inflammation, including autoimmune disorders, inflammatory bowel disease, and cancer. A recent study demonstrated that people who spent time in the forest had lower levels of inflammation than those that lived in the city. Even elderly patients who spent a week in the woods had reduced signs of inflammation.

Every once in a while, be a kid and take off your dang shoes. I will tell you, this is the one thing I miss the most living in Arizona (cacti, scorpions, and bare feet do not mix). Growing up in Maine, I would spend most of the summer shoeless. There is nothing better than walking on the beach or through the grass, feeling the earth beneath you.

And come to find out there are a lot of reasons for my love of my feet against the earth. I mentioned that we are 60% water, which allows us to conduct electricity. The earth has a negative ionic charge, and when we are barefoot, we are grounding our body to that charge.

Negative ions reduce our inflammation and detoxify us, including synchronizing our hormones and physiological rhythms. And those negative ions are most strongly conducted by the water. Next time you are near the ocean or a lake or a river or a creek, take the time to slip off your shoes and embrace the experience.

Are you struggling with insomnia? Ancient people believed that walking barefoot in the grass was the ideal cure for it!

Watch Your Inputs

You are made up of what you absorb. I will ask you to consider all of your senses once again. What are you seeing, hearing, feeling, smelling, and tasting? It is these things that become an intrinsic part of you. This has been addressed throughout the book, but I ask you to be incredibly mindful of your inputs:

- Are the people you spend the most time with positive or negative? Do you feel uplifted and motivated or depleted after spending time with them?

- What are you listening to? Is it growing you and motivating you or stagnating you?

- How are you nourishing your body? Garbage in, garbage results. Be mindful of your eating habits and how your body feels when you eat certain foods.

- Have you been able to identify specific scents that improve your focus and mental clarity?

- Do you have pictures or images around you that are motivating to you, and that allow you to feel joy?

We are a great big, walking intake valve, and we are pulling from every single thing that we exposed to each hour of the day. Be sure what you are taking in is serving you.

To Serve is the Greatest Honor

In 2006, I had the opportunity to travel to India for an extended work trip. Having never been to India and knowing that I was going to be responsible for onboarding a team of Indian employees, it was important to me that I understood their culture. To do so, I requested a visit to the local city market in Bangalore, despite being urged against it. It was not, I was told, a tourist destination.

The market was incredibly overwhelming and was indeed an assault on all of my senses. The brilliant color of spices collided with the dirt and dust. The sound of the crowds of people speaking an unfamiliar language was punctuated with the sound of cows and other animals. Seeking relief from the chaotic scene and the relentless sun, I ducked under a concrete overhang.

It was there that women were sitting with these large, woven mats covered in the most beautiful flowers I had ever seen. The smell of jasmine was intoxicating, and a welcome relief from the other not-so-nice smells of the market. The women were selling their flowers and gently creating leis for the Hindu temples.

One particular woman caught my eye. I estimated that she was probably in her late 70s or older, no teeth, and from the looks of it, she did not have much of anything at all. In front of her was a pile of flowers, and I watched as she carefully strung them together.

I did not speak her language, so I simply pointed to the flowers and attempted to hand her my money. She looked me up and down and then shook her head and hands at me.

I was devastated! Here I was trying to understand and assimilate to the culture, and I had managed to insult this poor woman. I had obviously violated some cultural rules.

To help me with the situation, I found my guide and asked him to please talk with her and fix the situation. He went over to talk with her and, after a few minutes, waved me over. As I neared, the woman gingerly got up, holding a beautiful lei. And with her arthritic hands, she pinned that lei in my hair.

Brimming with gratitude, I once again attempted to hand her my money. And once again, she waved me off.

"I do not understand," I pleaded with my guide, "why won't she take my money?"

"You do not understand." He responded kindly. "You see, your debt is paid in full. She does not want your money because you honored her by choosing *her* flowers. That is so much more valuable than any money you could give her."

That moment had a lasting impact on me. Again, I had always defined my worth and my value by my accomplishments. But this changed my perspective.

I kept that lei preserved in my journal. I still have it. It is brown and wilted, but it reminds me of a time when I met the richest woman in the world who had no material goods.

It was not long after that trip that I quit my corporate job to focus on serving others, recognizing that service is the highest honor and is the most gratifying of all pursuits.

You do not have to go to India to feel the profound impact of serving. Think about a cause that is uniquely personal to you and where you have passion. Identify opportunities to serve and to give back.

My best friend volunteers her services at a recovery center. Another dear friend collects personal care items and provides them to the homeless. And yet another works with veterans, helping them find hope and jobs after serving our country.

I volunteer with the local chapter of the National Speakers Association because it is important that I give back to an organization that has given me so much. And I genuinely love it.

When you serve, you will be richly rewarded. Of this, I am sure.

Habit #24: Identify an organization or cause that you are particularly passionate about and identify opportunities to serve.

Self-Love

Yes, I saved this for the last aspect of growing your gratitude. But not because it's the least important. But instead, because it is the most important. And the roots of self-love in this book go back to the first section when I discussed your beautiful brain, your mind, and your heart.

I know I've used this as an example before, but that is because it is just so appropriate!

You have to put on your oxygen mask before you help anyone else. My dear friend, I cannot emphasize this enough. And honestly, if this is the only thing you take from this book, I will rest easy knowing I gave you the most beautiful, perfect, awesome gift because YOU are the most beautiful, perfect, awesome gift to this world and to all of those that cross your path.

Unfortunately, things happen. We receive messages from people who don't love themselves, let alone love us. Their hurts become our hurts. And we carry those messages with us, like a bag of cinder blocks, heavier and heavier.

Today is the day you start getting rid of those cinder blocks. Because you are wonderfully made, and the only way you will shine and be fulfilled is when you know that with every fiber of your being.

No more of this less than shit. You are not less than anyone or anything. You are exactly what you are supposed to be, and that is a vehicle of love.

You have a right to make mistakes. Because they aren't really mistakes, are they? They are just feedback telling us we need to adjust and try again. Here are your rights:

- You have a right to grow, change, and mature.
- You have a right to love and be loved.
- You have a right to set healthy boundaries.
- You have a right to have bad days. And good days. And freaking awesome days.
- You have a right to take care of yourself as only your inner guidance system can tell you how to do it.
- You have a right to love the shit out of every single day of your life. No. Scratch that. You have a right to love the shit out of every second of your life.

So let's start right now. I want you to list ten things that you love about yourself.

1. _____
2. _____
3. _____
4. _____
5. _____
6. _____
7. _____

8. _____

9. _____

10. _____

Now repeat this process by listing ten additional things your friends, family, and co-workers love about you.

1. _____

2. _____

3. _____

4. _____

5. _____

6. _____

7. _____

8. _____

9. _____

10. _____

As my Uncle Reggie reminded me, I am reminding you:

You are too precious to waste.

You are a beautiful, wondrous creature, and you deserve to love the shit out of your life.

Key Take-Aways From Step Eight

1. Although we are physiologically wired to focus on the negative, it is possible to retrain our brain to focus on the positive

2. Being mindful, focusing on something positive and focusing on our breathing, improves our pre-frontal cortex

3. Practice gratitude daily, especially in writing

4. Create your affirmations and mantras and use them frequently

5. Embrace meditation as a gift that you are giving to yourself

6. Get outside and into nature whenever you can – and take off your shoes and feel the ground beneath you

7. The highest honor is to serve, and that service is returned ten-fold

8. LOVE YOURSELF

STEP 9: ESTABLISH

BUILD YOUR TRIBE

I had someone advise me recently not to use the word "tribe." They told me it was insensitive and offensive to indigenous people. To me, the term "tribe" was a beautiful word, so I was a little surprised. I perceived it as a word that represented something even better than family because it was much more inclusive. A tribe has your back. They are there for you. They will defend and protect you. These are all very positive things. But it made me curious to see where there was an offense.

I have three nieces that are Native American and a group of friends that are from various Native American tribes. It was over lunch one day that I asked one of these friends about using the word. In context, her family resides on the reservation ("the Rez"), and she visits frequently. Instead of taking exception with it, she found it complimentary. It is used in the highest of regards, with a very personal and protective sense to it. This was an honor for her and her family.

It does not mean that people that use the word 'tribe' to describe their chosen group fully understand what it is like to be Native American, but it does have an entirely positive connotation. To her, this was much more respectful than some other views of Native Americans.

While I did not need her validation, nor do I believe she represents all Native Americans, it made me feel better to know that how I interpreted and used the word was in alignment with how she felt.

Throughout this book, my ultimate goal is to be real. I swear when I feel I need to swear. I am transparent to my struggles when I thought that it added an element of relatedness and demonstrated a point. I do not worry about being politically correct. I am much too focused on serving and helping people by being authentic. I am not here to blow smoke up your ass. Not my gig.

So there you have it. I will continue to use the word tribe because I cannot imagine my life without my tribe. And it only has the most completely positive affiliation when I use that word. Hopefully, if it offends you, you can see there was positive intent.

We Need A Tribe

I'm going to be completely honest on this one, my friends. This is probably the hardest chapter for me to write. But it is so incredibly important that I could not possibly skip it.

While it is the sum and synergistic total of the nine GET IT DONE steps that will transform your life, there is an essential criticality to Step Nine – Establish.

I compare it to establishing seeds in fertile ground that will return a bounty for years to come. You are creating your root base, your foundation, and your strength. We were not meant to move through life alone, and it is no less critical today than it was in ancient times.

It has taken me 50 years, yes, that's five decades, to understand and appreciate just how important it is to develop your tribe. Not just any tribe. Your tribe. The *right* tribe.

Ironically, as a psychology person, I should know this! After all, many species increase the odds of survival when they band together and create greater mass and a more prominent presence. Think of that herd of antelopes on the savannah as the lionesses are contemplating their dinner. The herd sticks together. They do not scatter. If Mr. or Ms. Antelope decided that they would be better off alone, guess what? They would be swimming in the digestive juices of a lioness before they could blink.

Being in a group, a tribe, a herd, is one of our core survival mechanisms, but there is so much more to it than just numbers.

We must consider the quality of the herd, matching goals and qualities.

Picture it this way... you are a super-cool antelope, and your primary goal is to continue to move to find fresh new grass to chew on. But you end up hanging out with a herd of antelopes that does not like change. They want to hang out in one spot and stare at the barren ground, hoping new grass will spring up.

So maybe your curiosity gets the best of you... you wander away to find new green grass.

POUNCE! You're alone, and the lioness has you in her sights.

What does your tribe look like? Are they stuck in one place? Are they pacing with you? Do they allow you to grow?

My Tribes

I was an awkward kid. I was just different. I preferred hanging out in the woods over having a conversation with kids my age. I was nerdy smart and a social misfit. I had no real idea of how to engage with kids because I was lost in my own world. I had nothing cool to offer them. Sports was a no-go: I was terrified of the ball and had absolutely no eye-hand coordination. I read books and talked to animals. And worked. That was pretty much me in a nutshell.

I also had a sense from a young age that I did not need anyone and being alone and independent was a sign of strength. This was something reinforced by the way I was raised. My parents did not have friends. We did not have a tight-knit, close family. We really did not do things together, so my only reality was of being alone.

Which is why my most treasured times in childhood were when I would spend every other weekend with my dad and stepmother and get to hang out with my stepbrother and their family. They did things together, and it was awesome. Back home, I was relatively isolated.

I finally got my first real "best friend" when I was nine years old. We had just moved into a new house in a new neighborhood. As I was out riding my bike, I spotted a home on my street with a girls' bike. Yes! There must be a girl there my age. Maybe we could be friends?

After a few days of riding back and forth in front of the neighbor's house, I struck gold. A girl of my age was standing at the end of the driveway, wearing a bathing suit, wrapped in a towel, a perky ponytail on the side of her head. It took every ounce of hutzpah I could gather to stop and talk to her.

But I did! She WAS my age and in the same grade.

"My sister is taking me down to the river to swim. Wanna go?" she asked. Always the cautious one, I asked how old her sister was. "Twelve" was the timid response. "Yes, I'll go. But I'm going to tell my mother that she's 14, ok? Just in case she's worried". But honestly, my mother wasn't going to be worried. Parents weren't as concerned back in the 70s as they are now. But I didn't want to risk my chance to make a friend.

And with that, we became "best friends." I loved Stacie, and yet she annoyed me at the same time. She slept in late, and I was always up and early. She hated doing chores, and I liked doing them. She wasn't impressed with her family dinners, and yet, I thought they were the most fantastic thing ever. I loved and envied their family. It was warm and loving and normal. Not like mine.

But as teenagers do, we drifted apart for several reasons. I honestly take responsibility for that. I became distracted. I made poor choices. I did not prioritize our friendship.

Our 21st years couldn't have been more different. She was studying to be a marine biologist, and I was escaping an abusive relationship and had recently given birth to my third child. But we met up at a local bar, enjoying our freedom and the ability to purchase a drink legally.

As it happens, we found ourselves in the ladies' room together. I had a few drinks in me, as did she. And I took the time, right there amidst the stalls, to tell her how much I loved her and how much she meant to me. I probably looked like a silly, emotional, and slightly tipsy girl. She just gushed and told me she knew that I loved her, and she loved me as well.

That was July. It was her 21st birthday. I love that memory.

She called me in October on my 22nd birthday – we always talked on our birthdays. It was the last time I would ever hear her voice.

She was killed on December 22nd by a drunk driver.

That experience convinced me that I did not need friends. What was the point? They leave, they are killed, they do not understand you. I had priorities: my kids and my career.

I had managed to hang on to one friend from high school, Kim. (I've talked about her throughout this book because she is now and always will be *my person!*) She was loyal; she was there for me. Why would I need any others? So I just kept Kim. That posed a bit of a challenge when I left Maine and moved to Arizona, but we did not let the 2,700 miles come between us.

For the next 23 years, I had my one friend. I mean, I had some acquaintances, but no pick-up-the-phone-and-go-somewhere friends. Yes, that is correct. It is not a typo. It took me 23 years before this idea of having friends would once again surface. And ironically, it was because of a very similar tragedy.

January 2014, a young mother went out for a training run in Richmond, Virginia, with her husband, a local police officer. A doctor, driving under the influence, hit her. Meg Cross Menzies was killed instantly.

I saw the article on Facebook, and because of the connection with another senseless death due to a DUI, I became emotionally engaged. It just happened that I was at one of the lowest points in my life. One of my businesses had just failed, and I was dealing with a health crisis. I knew I needed to get my life back on track, regain my strength, and build my health. I joined the Facebook group and vowed to run on January 18th in her honor.

I wasn't a runner. In fact, I could barely walk at that time. And I absolutely hated running. But now I had a cause, a reason, and some emotional motivation.

This isn't about me running, although that has been an enormous blessing in my life. This is about the tribe I found through that group. A tribe of passionate, driven, caring, loving, and encouraging people; from all backgrounds, all over the world. The common thread of tragedy bonded us in an almost overwhelming way.

And my tribe started to grow. I had friends. People I truly loved, and they loved me. I got stronger. I got kinder. And I got more engaged in living a life of meaning.

But it didn't stop there. A few years later, my tribe more than doubled in size at a professional conference.

After years of speaking at events to promote my training company, I realized that it would be appropriate to enhance my professional competencies around public speaking. As one does in today's world, I used The Google (as my mother would say), searching "professional speaker."

That Google search led me to discover the National Speakers Association. I purchased a membership and signed up to attend the NSA annual conference, "Influence."

While I would rate the act of networking as one of my very *least* favorite activities in the entire world, I was intrigued and motivated to grow my platform skills. Although I knew no one, I walked into that conference, committed to self-growth.

And the weirdest thing happened.

I talked to people. And I liked it. And I liked them. And they liked me. And it lasted for five whole days! Five days of liking people and having people like me. I felt like I had found an alternate universe. I was social, and I was comfortable. And I was learning so very much. So I kept those new friends long after the five days. I was plugged into a big, extended tribe of like-minded people. Many of my peers in NSA have become incredibly dear friends, that have enriched my life in so many ways.

I lost my stepfather on December 27, 2018, 13 months after losing my father. He was laid to rest with military honors, and I took the loss hard. At his burial, I was surrounded by my tribe from my running community and my speaking community. They loved on me, hugged me, and held me up when I just wanted to collapse into nothing.

They love me unconditionally, they challenge me, they cry with me, and they celebrate with me.

When I announced the official publication date of this book, I was inundated with messages of support, telling me they couldn't wait to read it. If that is not motivating, I don't know what is!

Growing Your Tribe

Remember, this book is about productivity and having a fulfilled life. I am not advising you just to go hog-wild trying to find a bazillion friends. Not at all. Quality over quantity.

Evaluate your life, personally and professionally. What does your tribe look like? Do you have opportunities to grow your tribe or enhance it by stepping outside your comfort zone?

Professional Tribe

Look at growing your professional networks, both inside and outside of your company. Consider your profession, title, and role, your industry, your city, your professional goals.

I did not consider myself a "professional speaker" before I joined the National Speakers Association. I chose to participate to grow my skills. Think about your current and ideal roles or job titles. Are there organizations that support that role or trade? For example, project managers should get plugged into their local Project Management Institute (PMI) chapter.

Local chambers of commerce present an excellent opportunity to learn about other businesses in your area and make some great connections. If you are an entrepreneur or franchise owner, affiliation with your local chamber can have a significant impact on your business. You can also consider other business development groups such as BNI or Polka Dot Powerhouse.

Personal Tribe

I want you to take a moment and consider every facet of you. Everything that makes you *you*. What makes you come alive? What do you enjoy doing? Where are your gifts? Your interests? Let those questions guide your tribe building.

If you are a mom, find local moms' groups that align with your parenting style. Do not try to fit a square peg in a round hole. My oldest daughter is part of a "crunchy mama" group. She loves it. It definitely would not have fit my parenting style when my kids were younger! Remember to listen to the internal navigation that you have.

Do you hike? Bike? Run? Do yoga? Connect with others with similar fitness habits. My youngest daughters always played hockey, and to this day, their best friends are still the people within the hockey community.

Maybe you like to knit, or sew, or write poetry, or are interested in becoming a botanist or a photographer. Check out The Google, Meet-Up, or Facebook Groups. You will learn all about the groups around you that share your interests. Go out on a limb and meet with people. What do you have to lose?

I talked earlier about the role of faith and spirituality. Are you a member of a faith that meets regularly? This includes churches, synagogues, temples, etc. If your religious institution offers get-togethers outside of regular worship services, GO! Meet people in a setting that is not as controlled.

You can also seek out people outside of your immediate congregation that shares your beliefs. Maybe you do not attend the same house of worship, but you have the same belief system. Awesome.

And then grow yourself even further by finding friends that do not share your beliefs! You will be amazed at how much richness that can add to your life.

As a trainer / public-speaker, we are told over and over and over again: "Do not talk about politics or religion."

I call bullshit on that. I think that is why we have a society ripe with intolerance. We need to talk about our differences. We need to be curious about our differences. We need to explore our differences. I guarantee this with every ounce of my being: this will only make us stronger.

I had the great honor of working in India for an extended period with a fantastic group of people. We were all different, and at first, we were hesitant with each other personally. But as we worked together longer, our trust and our friendship grew.

We sat around one evening talking: A Christian, a Catholic, a Muslim, a Hindu, a Jew, and an Atheist.

(Yes, it sounds a bit like the start of a bad joke.)

I have never learned more than I did in those few hours. We asked each other questions. We explored our curiosity. And you know what? We liked each other even more. We did not get offended. We were not closed off. We welcomed the discussion. And we realized just how very much we all had in common despite our different faiths.

Not to get all wishy-washy on top of an enormous soapbox, but I do wish that could be replicated in this world. What we could do together with some curiosity, understanding, and love. What a world this would be! Don't be afraid to step out of your comfort zone and talk to people. Especially those that may not look like you or believe like you.

Going to the Big D and I Don't Mean Dallas

Now that I've got you all fired up about finding friends and growing your tribe, I need to give you the big, fat caveat associated with that.

If you have a relationship that is not serving you, you may need to consider severing that relationship. I'm not saying divorce your spouse because she doesn't share your love of running, or he doesn't want to do needlepoint with you. I am going to tread very lightly on romantic relationship advice. It is most definitely not my wheelhouse!

But let's look at your tribe, your friends. Seriously consider the relationships. Are you the giver or the taker, or is it equal?

Ultimately, you want a tribe that challenges you, uplifts you, and supports you, but not in an unhealthy, co-dependent way. They should understand and accept you, and you should understand and accept them. If they are trying to change you (in a negative way) or you think you are going to change them, it is probably not a healthy relationship.

I've had to "divorce" two friends in the last ten years. Considering that I have a pretty big tribe, I think that's an acceptable attrition rate. The relationships were simply not healthy. It does not mean they are bad people, or I hate them; it merely means that I couldn't have a healthy relationship with them. I wish them well, send them light and love, and cut ties.

Deciding to divorce them was not an easy decision. I felt terrible and fell into a trap and cycle of guilt. But I started paying attention to my emotions. Not only when I was with them, but even after we had spent time together. It just was not working for me.

The Ones You Can't Divorce

My mother was notoriously negative. And she wasn't a quiet, private negative person. Oh no. She was loud and proud about being pissed off 99% of the time. And everyone around her would know when she wasn't happy. Not only did she tell them with her words, but her face also hid no secrets (yes, that is where I get it from).

I loved my mother despite her negativity, but I had to learn techniques for insulating myself against it, because it would permeate my being, oozing into my pores, finding its way to my heart. Which then impacted my moods and my results.

A good friend of mine had a toxic mother, so she shared her technique with me. Before she would go to visit her, my friend would envision that she was stepping into a big suit of bubble wrap. She would physically imitate zipping up the bubble wrap suit to "protect her aura and her soul."

Once she left her mother's, she would unzip the suit and step out, completely unimpacted by the toxicity just lobbed at her by her mother.

If you have toxic people in your life, you own your response to them. Develop strategies to protect yourself, my friend. Maybe it is just changing the subject, perhaps it is limiting time with them, or maybe it is having a direct conversation with them about their negativity.

But here is the thing: you are too precious to waste.

And life is too damn short.

Do not let someone else's negativity and toxicity rob you of your joy. You own your joy.

Key Take-Aways from Step Nine

1. You are not meant to be a nomad. You are meant to have meaning relationships and connections. Be deliberate about building your tribe.

2. Your tribe should make you a better person, challenge you, love you, and support you. And you, in return, do that for them.

3. Consider both personal and professional connections to be part of your tribe.

4. If a relationship is not serving you and it cannot be repaired, consider severing it.

5. If you cannot sever a damaging relationship, take proactive action on protecting yourself from the impact of that person.

Conclusion

First and foremost, I want to thank you for honoring me by reading my book. It is an honor that I treasure and do not for one-minute take for granted. You are my inspiration. I want us all to have gentle and fulfilling lives. My heart hurts for people that do not have joy in their life. And it hurts even worse for people who do not even realize that they don't have joy in their lives.

This nine-step process allows you to change your life in remarkable ways. It is not easy. It is going to hurt. That is how you know it is working.

It is physically, emotionally, and physiologically impossible for us to make significant changes without discomfort.

Give yourself some grace, my friend. You may do a lot of zigging and zagging along your path to fulfilled and intelligent productivity. Remember, the zigs and the zags are just feedback. They are not failures.

Listen to your intuition, your soul, the core of you. Deep inside you, you know the kind of life you want.

And you deserve that life.

Remember that I am here, and I am your biggest cheerleader!

Now close this book and get SHIT done!

KEY TAKEAWAYS

Step One - Goals

1. Take time to consider how you want to live your life and how you want to be remembered.
2. Your goals and personal mission statement become your GPS.
3. Visualization is the most powerful step in creating the ideal life.
4. Listen to the emotions that are coming from your internal voice, your navigation system.

Step Two - Environment

1. Create an environment that minimizes sensory distractions. Turn off notifications and chimes. Reduce the number of windows you have open on your browser.
2. Do an inventory of your sensory sensitivities to stimulate productivity: visual, auditory, kinesthetic, olfactory, and gustatory.
3. Conduct a personal scan of your emotional distractions. Walkthrough the process to either destroy them or resolve them.
4. Practice meditation, in whichever form works best for you.
5. Be aware of your posture, including with your cell phone or other devices, and the amount of time that you spend sitting.

Step Three - Time

1. Prioritize creating healthy sleep habits. Do not start the week in a deficit by altering your wake-sleep patterns on

the weekend. Stick to a consistent wake-up time whenever possible.

2. Allow your circadian rhythm to dictate your energy allocation during the day, scheduling activities based on your peaks and dips.

3. Hydrate, hydrate, hydrate. Do so consistently throughout the day, making allowances for changing circumstances, such as sleeping, traveling, workouts, heat, etc.

4. Understand the power and connection with your posture, both psychologically and physiologically. Don't worry – you won't look like you have a stick up your butt. I promise!

Step Four - Insulate

1. Once you have identified and created your ideal environment for productivity, viciously protect it! My youngest daughter is a hockey goalie, and one of my proudest mom moments was when another parent commented that my girl was like a vicious bulldog on a short chain protecting her crease. Yes! Be a vicious bulldog!

2. Identify your most damaging distractions and put a plan in place to counteract, minimize, or eliminate those distractions.

3. Periodically conduct an emotional scan. What do you have brewing beneath the surface, and it is something that may be able to be resolved? If so, deal with it directly. If not, let it go.

4. Remember that you are always in control of your emotions. You cannot control the situation. You cannot control other people. But you can control your reaction and response.

5. Say "No" – loud and proud!

6. Embrace the zigs and the zags. They are feedback, not failures.

Step Five – Take Control

1. Neuroplasticity allows us to create new neural pathways in our brain, which then enables us to retrain our brain.

2. Dopamine is what allows us to feel pleasure. To hack your dopamine: celebrate the small wins with incremental goals, write down your accomplishments, define what is next, eat healthily, and practice health habits.

3. Serotonin maintains our mood balance. To hack your serotonin: create a positive emotional state, get outside, meditate and re-live happy moments, eat food high in trytophans, and write in your gratitude journal.

4. Oxytocin is our love and intimacy hormone. To hack your oxytocin: give someone a handshake, share a hug with receptive partners, and give gifts.

5. Endorphins are our natural analgesic. To hack your endorphins: Laugh, eat dark chocolate and spicy foods, and use aromatherapy.

6. One of the greatest gifts you can give yourself, mentally and physically, is a consistent regimen of exercise, at least 30 minutes per day.

7. Emotional intelligence is the ability to understand your emotions and control them, while understanding and having empathy for others' emotions. Know your triggers and identify actions to employ when they are present.

Step Six - Destroy

1. You are not good at multitasking. No one is. If you think you are, I am here to tell you, you are not. Sorry.

2. Multitasking robs us of cognitive functioning, creativity, emotional intelligence, and lowers our IQ.

3. Put your damn phone down when you are driving.

4. We have become addicted to distractions. We are literally distraction-junkies that feed on the release of dopamine when we get distracted.

5. The to-do list needs to be replaced with microbites of work.

6. You will work on one microbite at a time before tackling the next microbite.

7. You can only unlock the vault holding your to-do list when your current microbites are completed. At that time, you are welcome to reprioritize what is remaining on your list.

8. Conducting daily retrospectives, in writing, allows you to make adjustments to fine-tune your work and your prioritization approach.

9. Daily stand-ups create healthy tension and stress to engage us in getting the highest priority work completed in a timely fashion.

Step Seven - Optimize

1. Become very consciously aware of what you are prioritizing by not prioritizing.

2. When choosing to avert your attention from someone or something, call yourself out on it verbally.

3. Be kind to and engage service workers: smile, have a conversation, remember your manners.

4. Cluster sets of habits into multiple blocks throughout your day.

5. Use a Pomodoro Technique or something similar to chunk out your focus time.

6. Kill unproductive meetings.

7. Practice productive multitasking, overlaying autonomic tasks with something stimulating.

Step Eight - Notice

1. Although we are physiologically wired to focus on the negative, it is possible to retrain our brain to focus on the positive.

2. Being mindful, focusing on something positive and focusing on our breathing, improves our pre-frontal cortex.

3. Practice gratitude daily, especially in writing.

4. Create your affirmations and mantras and use them frequently.

5. Embrace meditation as a gift that you are giving to yourself.

6. Get outside and into nature whenever you can – and take off your shoes and feel the ground beneath you.

7. The highest honor is to serve, and that service is returned ten-fold.

8. LOVE YOURSELF.

Step Nine - Establish

1. You are not meant to be a nomad. You are meant to have meaning relationships and connections. Be deliberate about building your tribe.

2. Your tribe should make you a better person, challenge you, love you, and support you. And you, in return, do that for them.

3. Consider both personal and professional connections to be part of your tribe.

4. If a relationship is not serving you and it cannot be repaired, consider severing it.

5. If you cannot sever a damaging relationship, take proactive action on protecting yourself from the impact of that person.

Belinda Goodrich

HABIT LIST

Habit #1: Tune in frequently to your internal guidance system: your intuition, your emotions, your gut. And always trust it.

Habit #2: Consistently evaluate your physical environment to make adjustments in alignment with your preferred sensory inputs.

Habit #3: Practice conducting an emotional scan regularly to deal with shit that is distracting you.

Habit #4: Meditate daily in a way that works for you!

Habit #5: Set your alarm for the same time seven days per week. And don't dawdle in bed. Jump out of that bed, like a shark on a mission. Get up and do something. Have a cup of coffee. Write in your journal. Watch the sunrise. Do something.

Habit #6: Identify your natural circadian rhythm and then manage your day and your tasks to align with that rhythm.

Habit #7: Drink the recommended ounces of water per day, adjusting for situations that may require you to increase your intake. Start the day with a nice, refreshing glass of water!

Habit #8: Every 25 minutes, do a posture check. Take in a nice deep breath and straighten up. Envision yourself, opening up with confidence, and sending vital oxygen to your body and brain. And notice how confident you feel!

Habit #9: Commit to putting your oxygen mask on first before helping others. Repeat after me: "Just Say No!"

Habit #10: When things don't go as planned, do not assess it as a failure. Reframe it as simply feedback.

Habit #11: Identify when you have a mental and emotional shift toward negativity and take steps to hack the hijack immediately.

Habit #12: Move your body for at least 30 minutes per day. Dance, walk, skip, hula hoop. Whatever you enjoy.

Habit #13: Stay in touch with your emotions and your reactions to various triggers. Consider pursuing further learning about emotional intelligence.

Habit #14: Allocate blocks of time on your calendar for your focused work. Start brief and gradually increase that time. During the block, close out any internet browsers, email accounts, and turn off notifications on your phone.

Habit #15: Do not keep a long to-do list visible to you throughout the workday. Focus on microbites, small tasks, completing one at a time.

Habit #16: Conduct your personal retrospective in *writing*. Yes, actually handwrite it in a journal or notebook. The act of handwriting helps us create those new neural pathways I have been talking about throughout this book. When you handwrite the good things that are happening and those that you are going to change, you are literally writing them onto your brain and into existence.

Habit #17: At the start of each workday, increase your gratitude and accountability by acknowledging what you accomplished the previous day and what you will achieve during the current day.

Habit #18: Verbalize, yes out loud, that you are prioritizing whatever it is you are doing over another task or action that you believe you probably should be doing. That verbal acknowledgment may be enough to shift your attention and encourage you to make a different choice.

Hint #19: During transactions, put your phone aside and actually talk to the person taking care of you, smile, and say thank you. And put your cart in the cart corral when you are done shopping. #Karma

Habit #20: Break up your workday into 2-hour chunks of work, using the 25/5 system. Set a timer and close off any distractions. If you have a peer or co-worker on the same schedule, consider creating an accountability partnership with them, using the same system.

Habit #21: Control your calendar proactively, not allowing your calendar to control you. Eliminate unnecessary meetings. Block your work time first.

Habit #22: Use the time you devote to rote tasks to productively multitask.

Habit #23: When you see something that makes you happy, stop everything else, and allow yourself to focus on it for 20 to 30 seconds.

Habit #24: Identify an organization or cause that you are particularly passionate about and identify opportunities to serve.

Belinda Goodrich

ABOUT THE AUTHOR

Globally recognized as a productivity, project and change management expert, Belinda Goodrich is the founder and CEO of Goodrich Learning Solutions, PM Learning Solutions, and Goodrich Publishing.

Belinda grew up in her parents' small business, fostering an entrepreneurial spirit and approach from an early age that has lent to her success through multiple business endeavors. At the age of 18, Belinda opened a business in direct competition with her parents, achieving year-over-year growth.

With a focus on industrial and organizational psychology, Belinda studies the mind, emotions, and behaviors of business leaders and employees, and she leverages that knowledge to bring practical information and real-life solutions to stimulate business growth and productivity.

The author of multiple books and courseware on project management and PMI exam topics, Belinda is an in-demand facilitator, speaker, and consultant. The first woman in the world to achieve five of the PMI credentials, Belinda now holds the following: PMP®, CAPM®, PMI-SP®, PMI-ACP®, PMI-RMP®, PgMP®. Also, Belinda is a Certified Scrum Master.

Belinda is the author of Kick Ass Project Manager, CAPM® Exam Prep Study Guide, PMP® Exam Prep Study Guide, and multiple other project management exam preparation titles. She is a co-author on You@Work and Belinda received a Quilly® Award for her best-selling, co-authored book *The Will to Win* with famed leadership experts Jim Cathcart and Brian Tracy.

Belinda is the innovator behind the Intelligent Productivity Quotient™, an assessment of an individual's strength in navigating distractions and disruptions to apply an intelligent selection process for an activity or task choice.

Belinda is the Vice President of the Arizona Chapter of the National Speakers Association.

In her personal time, Belinda spends time outside, hiking, running, and talking to the local wildlife. She is a travel junkie and treasures exploring the world with her best friend. A self-diagnosed bibliophile, Belinda loves helping people connect with their stories through writing their own books. She is the proud mother of three daughters and has been richly blessed with six grandchildren.

Follow Belinda

Join the **BeGood Tribe** and connect with Belinda on her various social media accounts:

Facebook: facebook.com/TheBeGoodrich/

Instagram:.instagram.com/thebegoodrich/

LinkedIn: linkedin.com/in/belindagoodrich/

Twitter: twitter.com/TheBeGoodrich

Engage Belinda

Are you seeking to engage and transform your team, employees, or attendees with proven techniques to improve outcomes, productivity, and communication? Belinda is a professional member of the National Speakers Association and works with organizations and meeting professionals to ensure an engaging, practical, and results-focused outcome.

Belinda is available as a keynote speaker, consultant, and educator. Learn more about Belinda at BelindaGoodrich.com and on her YouTube channel.

Goodrich Learning Solutions, previously known as PM Learning Solutions, offers customized and timely training and employee development programs to organizations around the world. Goodrich Learning Solutions is focused on delivering first-class quality learning programs, both on-demand as well as classroom settings.

Popular offerings include:

- Emotional Intelligence Intensive Workshop
- Internal Customer Service Excellence
- Creating Raving Fans through Customer Service Excellence
- Effective Presentation and Facilitation Skills
- Project Life: Achieving Health and Balance with Work and Home
- Get It Done: Maximizing Productivity with Behavioral Hacks
- Project Management Fundamentals
- Engaged for Excellence: Virtual Teams Reinvented
- Agile Project Management
- Project Risk Management

Contact Goodrich Learning Solutions for your employee development needs. Info@GoodrichLS.com

GoodrichLearningSolutions.com

G OODRICH
PUBLISHING
DISCOVERING POTENTIAL

With a core value and belief that everyone has a story that the world needs to hear, Goodrich Publishing is a boutique publishing firm focused on giving a voice and a process to authors struggling with:

- Getting their book written
- Getting their book published
- Getting their book noticed

At Goodrich Publishing we meet the author where they are, providing services and support to make their story a reality. With an affordable services structure and one-on-one attention, Goodrich Publishing demystifies the publishing process and creates a fulfilling writing and publishing experience for everyone: inexperienced authors through multi-published authors.

Our passion is enabling YOUR story!

Contact us today: Info@GoodrichPublishing.com

GoodrichPublishing.com

Belinda Goodrich

www.ingramcontent.com/pod-product-compliance
Lightning Source LLC
Chambersburg PA
CBHW031129090426
42738CB00008B/1020